Happily
Ever
After

Also by Karen Linamen

*Pillow Talk: The Intimate Marriage from A to Z*

*The Parent Warrior: Doing Spiritual Battle for Your Children*

*Working Women, Workable Lives* with Linda Holland

*Deadly Secrets* with Keith Wall

# Happily Ever After

*. . . And 21 Other Myths about Family Life*

Karen Scalf Linamen

Fleming H. Revell
A Division of Baker Book House
Grand Rapids, Michigan 49516

© 1997 by Karen Scalf Linamen

Published by Fleming H. Revell
a division of Baker Book House Company
P. O. Box 6287, Grand Rapids, MI 49516-6287

Paperback edition published 1998

Printed in the United States of America

**Library of Congress Cataloging-in-Publication Data**

Linamen, Karen Scalf, 1960–
    Happily ever after : . . . and 21 other myths about family life / Karen
Scalf Linamen.
    p. cm.
    ISBN 0-8007-1741-4 (cloth)
    ISBN 0-8007-5675-4 (paper)
    1. Family. 2. Family—Religious aspects—Christianity. 3. Parenting—
Religious aspects—Christianity. 4. Parent and child. I. Title.
HQ734.L5658 1997
646.7'8—dc21                        97-14915

For current information about all releases available from Baker Book House, visit our web site:
                 http://www.bakerbooks.com

To
Minnie Lanham Scalf

———◆◆◆———

Nearly seven decades ago she accepted a blue polka-dot scarf from a seventeen-year-old boy smitten by love at first sight. They spent the next sixty-four years together, and the legacy of their loving marriage includes two children, five grandchildren, and eight great-grandchildren. Thanks, Mamaw, for giving life to this family. We love you!

# Contents

# Acknowledgments

y heartfelt thanks to everyone at Baker/Revell, especially Dwight Baker and the awesome Linda Holland. Many thanks as well to Twila Bennett and Marci DeVries for their promotional wizardry. I am also grateful to Sheila Ingram and the rest of the editorial staff, and to Traci DePree for her editing magic. Thanks also to Mary Wenger for her spit and polish.

I also want to express appreciation to Jan Johnson and Carol Bartosh for providing child care for my preciously distracting two-year-old during the final months before my deadline. In the same vein, Cherie Spurlock covered my car pool duties for months—I'm in her debt!

I am also grateful to all the women who let me pick their brains for anecdotes and ideas. Cherie, Nancy, and Melinda, our five-hour drive home from Houston stands out in my mind as a highlight! And never fear—the notes I took on that napkin are still intact. Stories that didn't show up in this book may well appear in the next!

Also, thanks to Sharon Kasachkoff, who brought me to tears with a rock (no, she didn't throw it at me) and encouraged me with her prayers.

And to my incredible parents, Gene and Geri Scalf, I'd like to say thank you for introducing me not only to the world, but to the magic of family life.

And last but most, I am thankful for my husband, Larry, who provided moral support as I completed this project, even though he was busy writing his own book at the same time (Advertisement: *Great* book on how to choose a college, published by Revell. Check it out!), and for my precious Kaitlyn and Kacie, who bring joy and meaning to my life.

# Introduction

"Children are what they eat."
"The best things in life are free."
"You can't take it with you."
We've all heard the sayings. But are they true? Correct me if I'm wrong, but it seems to me that when it comes to the wild and wacky world of family life, these sayings hold water about as well as a pair of panty hose.

After all, you and I both know that if children are what they eat, we'd all be raising Happy Meals. And if the best things in life are free, how come I'm always overdrawn? And it's obvious that whoever said you can't take it with you has never traveled with small children.

Many readers will remember that in my last book, *Pillow Talk*, I talked about emotional and sexual intimacy in marriage. It seemed only natural that I follow up with a book that focuses on one of the consequences of all that newfound emotional and sexual intimacy, meaning children.

Indeed, family life provides a broad spectrum of challenges, joys, blessings, and reasons to live near grandparents who will babysit for free. Characterized by heartache and hilarity and everything in between, family life is not for the faint of heart.

With this in mind, I decided to take on the task of examining twenty-two so-called myths about family life. What kind of myths? How about "Silence is golden," "Love means never having to say you're sorry," or "Father knows best"? As I examine these myths, and many others, I've combined humorous anecdotes, off-the-wall observations, and tried-and-true tips on everything from lethal lunch box leftovers to twelve ways to encourage uplifting communication in your home.

In the following pages, you'll read about:

- Myths and mysteries about pregnancy, including a discussion about the postnatal body. (The bad news is that the postnatal body is not a myth. The mystery is that women who have experienced it actually go on to have more children.)
- Etiquette for chronically tardy spouses who have yet to arrive at a movie theater in time to watch the previews, who have never heard the national anthem sung at a ballpark, and who believe the words "first come, first served" are discriminatory and should be struck from the English language.
- Child-safety devices that are not yet in existence, but should be.
- How to use humor to soften the blow of disappointment, crisis, and even tragedy.
- Thirteen things that a real superwoman would never be caught dead doing, along with a checklist entitled "You Might Be a Superwoman If . . ."
- Ten ways to say no to overcommitment.
- How to manage the exquisite tension that exists between keeping our kids safe and allowing them the

space they need to grow. Can we consistently provide both, or does the time ever come when we have to choose between the two?

- How to take better family photos and videos, including how to get rid of red-eye!
- The anatomy of a healthy apology, as well as five guidelines that will help you teach your children how to say "I'm sorry" . . . and mean it.
- Restaurant survival tips for parents of small children.
- And much, much more!

Our families are special, enriching our lives like nothing else on earth! Join me now in a celebration of family life designed to inform, inspire, and entertain, although not necessarily in that order!

## Myth #1

# Cleanliness Is next to Godliness

f cleanliness is next to godliness, then I may be in peril of losing my salvation.

The truth is that I am severely organizationally disadvantaged. It's not that I don't clean my house—indeed, I work hard at it. But even though I work *hard*, I am coming to the conclusion that I must not work *smart*. This is because, at any given moment, you'd be lucky to find one or maybe two rooms in my house that could be considered "company ready." On special occasions when I am, indeed, preparing for company, I might have as many as four rooms in tip-top shape. (Of course, the impact of this accomplishment wanes a little when you think about the fact that, counting bathrooms, I live in an eleven-room house.)

I wish that family life and housework were not so irrevocably linked. Unfortunately, if you have a family, you've got to have a place to put them. That means some sort of abode. And that means housework. Lately I've been pondering the injustice of the fact that I have to spend so many of my waking hours doing something at which I have so little skill. It seems to me that in most situations, if you get stuck with a job for which you have absolutely no aptitude, something eventually happens to save you. It's called getting canned. Sooner or later, someone who collects a bigger salary than you will call you into his office and point out the fact that you are a failure. He will then relieve you of your duties (and your paycheck). This is what happens in the real world. It's actually a good system.

When it comes to housekeeping, I am a failure. But no one ever relieves me of my duties. And there is no paycheck.

This is NOT a good system.

It's not that I'm not worthy of being fired. I mean, think about it: Pretend with me for a moment that you have hired a woman to cook for your family. This woman cooks in such a way that she uses the smoke alarm interchangeably with the oven timer. Let's pretend that last week she was browning hamburger when the smoke alarm began to squeal. Undaunted, she stirred the hamburger, turned on the exhaust fan, and left to set the table. The alarm continued to squeal, which was annoying although not altogether unusual just prior to mealtimes. It wasn't until she ambled back past the stove several minutes later that she noticed a dish towel on fire next to the hamburger.

*When it comes to housekeeping, I am a failure. But no one ever relieves me of my duties. And there is no paycheck. This is NOT a good system.*

You would relieve this woman of her duties, wouldn't you? Of course you would. I would, too. Unfortunately, Larry merely suggested that I try to be more careful next time.

What's the world coming to? Doesn't anybody have any standards anymore?

I would also fire a housekeeper who mixed the laundry and sent my husband to work wearing pink underwear.

I would fire any live-in who forgot to buy milk so often that my kids began to believe that Cheerios are actually *supposed* to be consumed with Cremora.

I would fire any domestic help who believed that one way to keep ants from attacking dirty dishes left overnight in the sink is to spray the kitchen counter with Raid (for the complete, unabridged confession on this one, see page 41 of my book *Working Women, Workable Lives*).

And yet no one fires me.

It's just not fair.

I would love to have a clean house. I would love to live in an environment...

*I would love to live in an environment where refrigerator leftovers don't stick around so long they start getting their own junk mail.*

... where dust bunnies don't double as the family mascot;

... where refrigerator leftovers don't stick around so long they start getting their own junk mail;

... where I could allow guests to roam free without wondering if they're peeking in my closets and worrying about lawsuits should they happen to become buried under the inevitable resulting avalanche.

Thank God that the condition of my house does not determine the condition of my soul. And yet, while cleanliness and godliness may not be as closely related as we are often told, there's still something to be said for being able to find a clean dish when you need one.

## New Motivations for Tired Homemakers

I could devote the remainder of this chapter to 101 housekeeping secrets designed to save you time and energy. And yet there are hundreds of books on the market that do just that. (I should know—I own roughly half of them. It makes me feel better knowing that the secret to organized living is somewhere on my bookshelves. Someday I may actually go looking for it.)

*Last month I managed to clean out two closets and hold a garage sale: I made $400. (I figure if I clean out the rest of my closets I can probably put one of my children through college.)*

So I'm not going to tell you *how* to clean your house. For those kinds of insights, pick up the latest book by Emilie Barnes or Sandra Felton or even Heloise.

I, on the other hand, am going to tell you *why* you should clean your house.

Sometimes, gaining a new perspective on something can make all the difference in the world. To that end, let me present to you the following perspectives with the hope that one or more of them might help you to see homemaking in a new light! After all, knowing that vinegar and water make a great window cleaner isn't much use if cleaning windows falls somewhere on your priority list below flossing the dog. To help you, here are seven new motivations for tired homemakers.

## Motivation #1: Mental Space

Despite the proliferation of "A Messy Desk Is the Sign of a Creative Mind" plaques in circulation, clutter does not enhance brainpower or creativity. On the contrary, clutter is distracting. I know this because I struggle with clutter. I don't mean that I tend to be a clutterer (although that would be an accurate assessment). No, I mean that every time I walk from one room to another, I struggle with clutter: toys, abandoned newspapers, discarded socks, old homework papers, last month's junk mail I still intend to read . . .

Sometimes I get the feeling my house is a little like the Eagles' Hotel California: Things check in but they don't check out. What kind of things? How about clothes that haven't been in style since I had to have my pet rock put to sleep, or my collection of Barry Manilow songs—on eight track—or the two dozen plaques I own that try to assure me that "A Messy Desk Is the Sign of a Creative Mind" (all gifts from friends who know me a little too well).

The only good thing about clutter is that, indeed, one woman's junk is another woman's treasure. Last month I managed to clean out two closets and hold a garage sale: I made $400. (I figure if I clean out the rest of my closets I can probably put one of my children through college.)

Like I said, garage sale profits are the single benefit. In every other way, clutter is a bummer. Living with clutter raises anxiety levels, creates feelings of guilt, and requires some level of justification or denial that saps mental energy from more productive pursuits. Clutter is distracting. Clutter sabotages concentration. Clutter does more than crowd your closets—it clouds your thinking as well.

In contrast, a tidy environment is soothing. It leaves room for your thoughts and imagination to cavort on subjects unrelated to housework. It's also easier to relax and rejuvenate in an organized environment.

The next time you're faced with unpleasant housekeeping projects, don't look at the task at hand as the end result of your efforts. Your labors achieve something more than a sparkling bathroom or an organized pantry: They can whisk away some of the sources of anxiety, stress, guilt, and distraction as well.

## *Motivation #2: Exercise*

I'll admit you're not going to lose thirty pounds keeping your kitchen floor waxed, but housekeeping can certainly be used to get your blood flowing and adrenaline pumping. The key is to pick up the pace. Mentally integrate the concepts of exercise and housework and make the effort to do things in a way that will benefit your body as much as it benefits your environment. Here are some suggestions:

- Crank up your stereo or CD player with good "moving" music. Choose something with a nice, fast beat to get you going.
- Wear comfortable clothes and good athletic shoes. Dress as you would if you were going to the gym.
- Establish a time limit and try to accomplish an aggressive housekeeping agenda in that period. For example, strive to mop the kitchen floor, vacuum the house, and complete two loads of laundry before nine o'clock.
- Work those muscle groups. Don't necessarily try to save energy or do things the easiest way. If you have to go upstairs, don't plod: run. Folding laundry? Don't sit in front of the TV and fold for the duration of your favorite soap. Dump the clothes on the kitchen table, stand as you fold, and try to get the job done as quickly as possible. Mopping the floor? Get aggressive. Work those muscles. Build up a sweat. You might even want to consider strapping one-pound weights on your wrists and ankles as you work.
- Create a regimen that reinforces the idea that you are doing these activities to exercise your body as well as enhance your home. Begin with some warm-up stretches. Stop when your "time limit" is up. Unwind with some cool-down stretches. Reward yourself with a cold drink or hot shower or both.

### *Motivation #3: Gratitude*

As a rule, my attitude about housework leaves a lot to be desired. In fact, it's safe to say that housekeeping makes me downright grouchy.

A few weeks ago, however, my ten-year-old daughter, Kaitlyn, undertook a homework assignment that left me feeling convicted regarding my frequent grumbles. She was asked to memorize a poem to recite to her class, and by the time she had selected the following poem and learned it by heart, I had heard it two dozen times and had it practically memorized myself. But more importantly, the words spoke to me, and I knew I would never be able to look at housework in quite the same way again. Here's the poem:

### I'm Thankful for Brushes and Brooms

I heard Mom say as she scrubbed today,
"I'm thankful for brushes and brooms.
I'm glad to clean my cozy house
That's filled with cheerful rooms."

I heard Mom say at the washing machine,
"I'm thankful for dirty clothes.
I'm glad that I have a healthy child
Who can play each day she grows."

I heard Mom say at the sink tonight,
"I'm thankful for dirty dishes.
I'm glad we filled our plates with food
Instead of empty wishes."

I heard Mom say in her prayers tonight,
"I'm thankful for problems today.
If life never got a little bit rough,
I might forget to pray."

V. Gilbert Beers

Just a simple kid's poem, but the message is potent. Do you want a new perspective on housekeeping? Try taping this poem where you can read it as you're washing dishes or folding laundry.

21

## Motivation #4: Accomplishment

A fourth motivation for tired homemakers is the sense of accomplishment that can be derived from the act of cleaning. No, I haven't been sampling the kitchen sherry, and yes, I really do believe that the act of cleaning can be therapeutic.

After all, when life is racing too quickly and frustrations abound and we're feeling overwhelmed with all that we've been given to do, what other pursuit can give us such a quick return on our investment of time and energy?

- If we're feeling blue and decide that losing ten pounds will pick us up, we're looking at one to two weeks of diligence before we'll be able to see any difference in our waistlines, and one to two months before our goal is realized.
- If we're feeling stymied and decide to return to college to finish an abandoned degree, we may be talking years before the diploma is in hand.
- If our environment gives us the blahs, it'll take at least the weekend to slap a coat of fresh paint on the walls, and several months to save up the money to buy some new living room furniture.

Most improvements we would like to make in our lives require weeks, months, and even years to be accomplished. And yet, when pressures mount and life seems at its most frustrating, there is something we can do that will yield results in, oh, three to five minutes (even seducing our husbands usually takes longer than that).

That's right. Make a beeline for the broomcloset, ladies, because while very little in life delivers near immediate results and gratification, cleaning does. Indeed, in less time than it takes to talk your husband into letting you have a turn with the remote control, you can enjoy a visible improvement in your environment and experience the pride and satisfaction that comes with accomplishment.

## Motivation #5: Your Family Will Feel Nurtured, Loved, and Cared For

They say that actions speak louder than words, and there's something about a picked-up home, casual order, clean bathrooms, underwear in the underwear drawers, and a hot meal that says "I care about you."

*I used to think of housework as "The Curse of the Mommies."*

Of course, maintaining that kind of environment is not easy for some of us. There are times I think my family should be able to bask in the knowledge that they are nurtured and cared for even as their home lies in shambles around them. It's been clean before, can't they remember what it looked like? Isn't it enough that I *tell* them they are cared for even as I suggest they wear yesterday's socks because the laundry hasn't been done in two weeks? Isn't it enough that I *tell* them they are nurtured even as I announce that dinner will be served ten minutes before bedtime, or as soon as I can find the can opener, whichever comes first?

Oh, sometimes it's okay to ask family members to cut us some slack. And it's more than okay to ask them to pitch in and help. But warm-fuzzies have short-term memories—and if we want our spouse and children to feel nurtured and cared for, our intentions need to translate into actions more often than not.

## Motivation #6: You Deserve It!

I used to think of housework as "The Curse of the Mommies." Lately I've been trying to think of dust cloths and the dishwater in a new light. After all, my spouse and kids aren't the only ones who feel more nurtured and cared for in a warm and orderly environment. I feel better, too! It's nice to be motivated to keep an inviting home for my family . . . but I need to do it for myself as well. Sure, it takes effort to wipe down the tub when I'm done, or hustle through the dinner dishes in time to browse a magazine before bed, or dust and organize my dresser top to make room for a bouquet of supermarket blossoms.

But in the words of Cybill Shepherd, "I'm worth it!"

### Motivation #7: Nobody Else Is Going to Do It

Okay, so I don't like this fact any more than you do. I keep holding out for the vacuum gnomes to make an appearance. I think they must have lost my address.

I was a new bride of one week when I conducted my first whirlwind cleaning tour through our home. I washed dishes, laundered clothes, scrubbed toilets, waxed floors. Proud with my accomplishments and pleased by my surroundings, I sat down to enjoy the fruits of my labor.

I was still sitting one week later when Larry, naked, hollered at me from the shower: "Karen! Do we have any clean towels or clothes?"

*I keep holding out for the vacuum gnomes to make an appearance. I think they must have lost my address.*

Looking around the house, I was in shock. Everything I had done had been undone. One week after I had labored, I was once again surrounded by dishes, laundry, dust, and debris.

All joking aside, I really was surprised. It had never dawned on me that housekeeping would be a regular part of my life as a married woman. I don't know what alternatives I thought there were—I guess I hadn't thought much about it at all. Someone else had taken care of those things for twenty-one years of my life.

Where's Mom when you need her?

Fifteen years later, I'm finally getting the picture. No one else is going to do these things. If that's not a motivator, I don't know what is.

I've often heard the saying, "If not me, then who? If not now, then when?" used in connection with loftier aspirations than picking up a dirty sock. But I think of it often as I cruise my home and spot things that need to be done.

So there they are, Seven New Motivations for Tired Homemakers.

| | |
|---|---|
| **M**ental Space | **F**amily nurturing |
| **E**xercise | **U** deserve it, and . . . |
| **G**ratitude | **N**obody else is going to do it! |
| **A**ccomplishment | |

Notice anything? Granted, housework may not qualify as MEGA FUN, but if we put a little effort into improving our attitudes about this unavoidable foundation of family life, we just might be surprised at the results.

 ## Our Best Housekeeping Tips

I asked five women to give me their best organizational tips, shortcuts, and secrets. Here's what I learned.

Sheila Cook, mother of two sons, ages 10 and 12: I keep a Master Grocery List in the drawer in the kitchen. I typed an alphabetical list of all the things we typically buy at the store, from apple sauce to Ziploc bags, and then made photocopies of the sheet. There's a box by each item, and my entire family knows to check the things they want me to pick up on my next trip to the market. My boys know, for example, that I won't be buying Gatorade unless it's marked. This way we all share the responsibility for keeping the home stocked with favorite foods and products, and I don't have to worry about forgetting something important.

Peggy Foster, mother of two daughters, ages 11 and 26: Clean one room at a time and don't stop until it's finished. If you find things that don't belong in that room and need to be put away elsewhere, don't leave the room. If you do, you may get distracted. Instead, keep a basket with you. Put all the odd items in the basket and put them away all at once after you've finished straightening the room.

Monica Riga, mother of one daughter, age 1: I spread my housework throughout the week rather than saving it up for the weekend when I could be spending time with my family. Monday through Wednesday I concentrate on laundry. On Thursday nights after work I spend less than an hour dusting and doing bathrooms. After work on Friday I vacuum the house and mop my kitchen floor. On Saturday I've got a clean house and can focus my attention on my husband and daughter.

Jeffie Burns, mother of three children, ages 12, 16, and 17: I have three kids, two jobs, and am working on my master's degree as well. To save time, I use paper bowls for breakfast cereal, sturdy paper plates for lunch and dinner, and paper cups all day long. After a meal, kitchen cleanup takes minutes. We just throw it all away! Using paper products costs me about twenty dollars a month. I used to spend an hour a day washing dishes. At twenty bucks a month, every dollar that I spend buys me more than an hour of my time. I'm worth it!

Geri Scalf, mother of three grown daughters: I keep duplicate cleaning supplies under every bathroom sink, and in the kitchen as well. That means four sets of paper towels, Windex, foaming cleanser, and toilet bowl supplies. When everything is right at hand, it's easy to open the cupboard and spend two minutes wiping down the mirror and sink. I'm not lugging supplies from room to room, and should I happen to run out of something in one bathroom, I've got backups throughout the house. Also, nix the cleaning rags. I use paper towels and toss them when I'm done. No laundry.

Karen Linamen, mother of two daughters, ages 2 and 10: Okay, so I had to put in my two cents worth. Piggybacking on my mom's idea above, I keep trash can liners right where I use them, rather than in a drawer or closet somewhere else. I drop the roll of bags into the bottom of my trash can before inserting a liner. When a bag is full, I lift it out, then reach inside the can or basket for the next liner.

## Myth #2

# Children Are What They Eat

 e've all heard the adage that "you are what you eat." If you have children, you know this cannot possibly be true. If it were, we would all be raising Happy Meals.

From birth on, the bond that children experience with their food is, if anything can be said about it at all, downright scary. In fact, the journey from breast milk to decaffeinated coffee is one fraught with perils, funny anecdotes, and plenty of epicurean experimentation (what else would you call it when a kid's favorite sandwich contains bananas and mayonnaise?). Indeed, the only thing missing from the interchange between kids and food seems to be nutrition.

As a mother of two, I sometimes dream about being the first to popularize the concept of whole grain and vegetable IV drips for children. But until that happens, I am faced with the challenge of, three times daily, trying to make sense out of the weird and wonderful relationship my kids enjoy with their food. And as I do, I find myself pondering the answers to questions like:

How do toddlers get any nutrients at all when the amount of food worn, flung, and dropped exceeds actual consumption twenty-five to one?

Why will one lima bean induce gagging and even vomiting when eighty-seven pieces of Halloween candy and four caramel apples will not?

Would someone please explain why so many of our kids' favorite foods are orange?

No doubt, if you share your home with offspring who are still too young to vote, your questions are similar to mine.

Perhaps you are preparing to lug an infant carrier into a restaurant for the very first time. Or maybe your thumbs have permanent mustard stains from the thousands of school lunches you have lovingly crafted so your child would have something to trade for two Twinkies and some Gummi Worms. Or it's possible that your teens have nagged you to the point that you're actually considering conceding that macaroni and cheese count as a yellow vegetable.

*Chicken fingers are the one thing that my two-year-old will consistently eat at a restaurant (besides the Cremora and Sweet'n Low).*

Whatever your situation, join me as we take a look at a few of the more intriguing facets of the relationship between children and their cuisine. Let's start with restaurant etiquette for small children. (If you have older kids, you have two options: You can read the next couple pages, remembering years gone by and laughing along with those of us still carrying Tommee Tippee cups into restaurants, or you can skip ahead to page 34 and discover some lunch box survival tips for moms of school-aged kids.)

## Eating Out with Small Children: Fun or Folly?

I've got a bone to pick with television actor Robert Stack. For years now, he's been keeping Americans busy pondering *Unsolved Mysteries* on subjects such as missing relatives, puzzling crimes, and alien beings from outer space. Meanwhile, some of life's more pressing mysteries are being completely neglected.

For example, I have it on good authority that parents across the nation are losing sleep at night wondering how so many restaurants can, with a clear conscience, serve an anatomically nonexistent food source to our children. I mean, even a city gal like myself knows that chickens don't have fingers. Yet there's not a restaurant this side of the moon that doesn't offer, somewhere on its menu, poultry digits.

And for good reason. Kids love them. My friend Cherie says that each Sunday after church, her ten-year-old daughter spouts heated convictions about which restaurant the family should patronize. One week Laura might beg for Don Pablo's Mexican Buffet. Another week she insists on Italian cuisine. Still another week she swears she won't settle for anything less than Southern fare at the Black Eyed Pea. And yet her fervor is puzzling because Laura's meal remains the same regardless of where the family dines. Surrounded by a mariachi band, or red-checked tablecloths, or even grits, Laura eats the same thing at every restaurant in the city.

You guessed it.

Chicken fingers.

I used to fight it. At one point I tried to get my daughter Kaitlyn, also ten, to order other things from the menu: hamburgers, spaghetti, even dessert. But nothing doing. And even I have to admit that chicken fingers are the one thing that my two-year-old, Kacie, will consistently eat at a restaurant (besides the Cremora and Sweet'n Low).

When it's all said and done, I guess the only thing to which I can really object is the price: At three bucks for three chicken fingers, two of which Kacie usually throws on the floor, this chicken doesn't come "cheep." Recently I started smuggling my own chicken fingers into restaurants. I discovered I can buy a bag of eighty frozen chicken nuggets from a warehouse discount store in my city (try a Sam's Club or Price Club near your home) for about seven bucks. I heat four nuggets in the microwave before heading out the front door, and let Kacie eat her brown-bag kid's meal at the restaurant. This way I get twenty Sam's Club "kid's meals" for less than the price of about three of the restaurant variety.

Yet eating out with kids—particularly small kids—can still be a challenge. How can we de-stress the experience, making it more fun than folly? I talked to some seasoned moms and gathered the following six suggestions which I call the Teapee Principles. Why Teapee? It's simple. To make these ideas easier to remember, I took the first letter of each of six principles and tried to arrange them into a word that made sense. Teapee may not make much sense but it was better than Eat Pee, which was my second choice and would be, as you can imagine, a disturbing title for a collection of suggestions regarding restaurant etiquette for small children.

So, here they are. The Teapee Principles for happier family dining:

**Timing**. This one might seem pretty obvious, but every mother I talked to mentioned it, so it must be pretty important. If you are the parent of small children, plan culinary excursions with your child's schedule in mind. When Kacie was an infant, I planned lunches with friends during nap time. By feeding Kacie before we left home, I was practically assured that she would fall asleep in the car on the way to the restaurant, where I would carry her car seat to our booth and let her snooze while I schmoozed. Now that Kacie's two, I plan restaurant trips around nap time, not during.

A friend of mine, Jill Loftin, is the mother of three children and a waitress at a local Chili's Restaurant. She echoes the sentiment regarding timing: "You wouldn't believe how many people come into the restaurant at 10:00 or 11:00 at night toting small kids. A tired kid in a restaurant is a formula for disaster."

Karan Willis, mother of three boys, had another idea related to timing. She suggested timing your meal to avoid restaurant rush hour. A crowded restaurant can mean having to wait to be seated, slower service once you're at your table, not to mention a larger audience if your kids decide to misbehave!

**Expectations.** Don't set your kids up for failure by expecting them to behave like adults. Make sure your expectations are consistent with the age of your child. Kids—particularly small kids—are going to spill milk and drop food and squirm when they're bored and complain when they're hungry. Jill admits that a pet peeve of hers is to hear a parent yelling at a kid for just being a kid. She says: "As a mom and a waitress, my best advice to parents is to make sure the needs of your small children are being met. If they're wet, change them. If they're hungry, get them something to eat right away. If they're bored, help them to feel entertained. Kids aren't adults. We can't expect them to handle hunger or boredom or discomfort the way a grown-up would."

**Attitude.** Sometimes, despite a parent's best intentions, everything goes wrong all at once. The food took too long and arrived cold. The baby filled his diaper and you forgot to bring diaper wipes. You're still mopping up your four-year-old's spilt milk when your toddler yanks the wig off the head of the woman sitting behind you. What is the one resource that may pull you through the moment with your sanity intact? Your attitude.

Jill says, "Some parents get so uptight, and others are smooth as silk. When kids are kids, some parents get in a pickle over it, and others just deal with the problem in a calm manner and go on with their meal." The key is to try to keep a sense of humor and remember that sometimes comedy is merely tragedy plus time. A decade from now, you and your kids will laugh about the time Junior slipped from your grasp during a diaper change and ran naked between the tables at Denny's.

**Preparation.** Experienced moms have reminded me that there's a lot that can be done to encourage a happy mealtime before you ever get to the restaurant. Going prepared with toys, crayons, juice, and snacks can make waiting for dinner to arrive a more pleasant experience. Diane Watson, a mother of four children ages nine months to nine years, even suggested practicing "restaurant manners" at home during certain meals to establish in young minds the kind of behavior that will be expected of them while eating out. This same friend told me that she and her husband will often help their children with menu decisions before the family ever de-vans. Particularly if they are about to visit a familiar restaurant, Dave and Diane will establish what everyone gets to drink and who wants cheese on their hamburgers and if any of the kids will be sharing a meal and what it is they're going to split. This saves time, hassle, and even money.

**Entertainment.** For young kids, entertainment might mean arriving at the restaurant with favorite toys. For older kids, it might mean engaging them in conversation or word games. Jill speaks of being impressed with one family of four that she observed one evening during her shift. The parents engaged their preteens in a quiet game of "I spy," providing an entertaining way to pass the time, as well as a warm memory for later years.

Before we added a new baby to our family, if Larry and I hoped to accomplish any communication during the meal, we let our second-grader invite a friend her age to join us. The girls entertained each other, and Larry and I were able to focus on our conversation relatively undisturbed.

My friend Karan suggested that, if you have small children, one parent can entertain them away from the table before the food arrives. She says, "My husband, Steve, will walk the youngest children around outside, looking at the fountain or the flowers or whatever. With little ones, it's sometimes helpful to minimize the time they have to sit quietly at the table."

*Sometimes comedy is merely tragedy plus time. A decade from now, you and your kids will laugh about the time Junior slipped from your grasp during a diaper change and ran naked between the tables at Denny's.*

**Environment**. Save the steak house for a night when the babysitter's free. Sometimes it pays to sacrifice atmosphere for a place that is a little more kid-friendly. Lately some of my family's most relaxing meals have been at a local McDonald's that boasts an indoor play area. I make sure to feed my toddler before we go, knowing that she will be too distracted once we get there to swallow a bite of dinner. While she plays, Larry and I can actually catch up on each other's week without having to pause the conversation every twenty seconds, or communicate sans eye contact because we're watching to make sure Kacie doesn't climb out of her high chair again.

**T**iming. **E**xpectations. **A**ttitude. **P**reparation. **E**ntertainment. **E**nvironment. Okay. So I never said eating out with small children was going to be easy. But it can be done, and done in such a way that the experience may actually be worth repeating (even if only during leap years or during appearances of Halley's comet).

## Beating the Lunch Box Blues

I hate making school lunches. The way I figure it, there should be a law against having to touch a slice of baloney at six forty-five in the morning. And why is it that the Tupperware lid that was relatively easy to locate after dinner is AWOL on any given school morning? And what about those Monday mornings when you realize that Friday's leftovers are lurking ominously in Junior's lunch box—the same lunch box that spent the weekend fermenting in the backseat of your van?

One morning I opened a lunch box that had spent Easter vacation in Kaitlyn's school locker, got a whiff of what was inside, and had to be rushed to my doctor's office for respiratory trauma. I was still wheezing, my throat swelling closed and my skin flushed with hives, when the doctor asked if I had eaten anything to which I might be allergic. I shook my head. The only thing I'd done that morning, I told him in a squeaky whisper, was crack open a lunch box ripe with last week's leftovers. The doctor nodded knowingly as he shot me full of Benadryl, which leads me to believe that he either has kids of his own, or that a lot of his patients are mothers of school-aged kids.

Of course, the only thing worse than making a school lunch is paying the $2.50 it costs to buy a hot meal at my daughter's school.

I've talked to a lot of parents about this, and it appears that making school lunches ranks about equal on everyone's list of favorite activities, somewhere between fishing a toddler's favorite stuffed animal out of the toilet and getting a speeding ticket.

And yet, being the optimist that I am, I believe it doesn't have to be this way. I believe there are things that you and I can do that will simplify the process of packing lunches for our school-aged kids. Here are several ideas:

1. Experiment with *creative solutions to boring meals*. My daughter thinks the sandwiches I make are boring. She's always begging for the expensive, exotic lunches her friends bring to school, like deluxe Lunchables that include lunch, drink, dessert—everything but tax and tip. One morning, tired of hearing the "boring lunch" complaint, I sent her to school with what I dubbed the Reese's Peanut Butter Sandwich: I

spread peanut butter on a Hershey's chocolate bar and put it between two graham crackers. She was thrilled.

Another day we brainstormed together to satisfy her yearnings for variety by sending a dill pickle wrapped in two pieces of baloney. One of my friends has discovered that her son simply salivates over flour tortillas spread with peanut butter and honey. Growing up, I knew a boy whose favorite sandwich contained strawberry jam and cream cheese.

*I've talked to a lot of parents about this, and it appears that making school lunches ranks about equal on everyone's list of favorite activities, somewhere between fishing a toddler's favorite stuffed animal out of the toilet and getting a speeding ticket.*

If your child is as bored eating lunch as you are making it, why not shake things up with the unexpected? Of course, I'm not suggesting that you abandon nutrition altogether, but in my book it's better to pack a fun lunch that your kids will eat than a healthy lunch that gets sacrificed to the humble abode of Oscar the Grouch. And remember, when you are crafting a creative lunch, keep in mind that your taste buds are not the final authority in this case! So go ahead . . . satisfy your son's cravings for that macaroni and cheese sandwich . . . your daughter's yearnings for apples dipped in ranch dressing. My hunch is that every kid has some weird food penchant that would help chase away the sack-lunch blues.

2. Another idea is to *create a school lunch command center.* I thought I was organized, keeping my sandwich bags with my other food wraps, the potato chips in the pantry with the rest of the snack foods, the thermos with my drinking glasses, and so on. Then it dawned on me that, to put together a single school lunch, I was having to open no less than a dozen separate cupboards and

36

drawers. If you traced my steps around my kitchen on any given school morning, you'd have a choreographical extravaganza to rival Tchaikovsky's Nutcracker Suite—the extended version.

I finally got smart and created a school lunch command center. Lunch boxes, sandwich bags, small storage containers, plastic forks, thermoses, napkins, and even a loaf of bread have been convened in one cupboard for easy access. On the counter below that cupboard, in plastic canisters, are what I call lunch box staples. One canister holds individual bags of potato chips. Another canister holds sweets (leftover Halloween candy, miniature candy bars, or individually wrapped cookies or brownies. Pre-wrap your own by putting some baked goodies—either store-bought or homemade—into plastic baggies). Next to the canisters sits a bowl of fruit: oranges, bananas, tangerines, apples (washed).

At 6:45 A.M., I open one cupboard for supplies, then grab a piece of fruit, bag of chips, and one dessert item and I'm nearly done. The only thing I have to think creatively about is a sandwich or other main item. Of course, to keep this system from becoming too predictable, you've got to go wild now and then with something really weird, like the suggestions for creative lunches in the previous section. But for a lot of school mornings, this system works great and can allow you to save your frustration for really important things, like when your son walks out the front door and remembers you're supposed to bring four dozen cookies to a classroom party in two hours.

3. Finally, don't be afraid to *solicit help from older children.* Each night, make your child responsible for packing his or her lunch box with non-perishable items: a piece of fruit, cookies, chips, napkin. In the morning, all you need to do is add the refrigerated items: sliced carrots, yogurt, sandwich, cheese sticks, drink, or whatever.

In addition, each day after school my ten-year-old has the responsibility of clearing her lunch box of leftovers and debris (which saves time on several fronts: I not only have less to do each morning, but I'm spending far less time at the doctor's office).

Let me just say that there is a magic key that is foundational to the success of any system that relies on children handling an element of responsibility. In fact, there is a single phrase, that—if you can remember it—will ensure the success of any endeavor in which you ask your child to belly-up to any given daily chore.

And no, the phrase I am thinking of is not "nag incessantly."

Instead, the phrase that you need to acquaint yourself with is, quite simply, "too bad."

Let's say it's Tuesday morning and you discover your son has not prepared his lunch box with cutlery, napkins, or edible lunch accessories. Rather than nag—or bailing him out by reaching for the cookie jar—simply evoke, in the privacy of your own mind, the magic phrase.

Think to yourself: "Too bad."

Then buck up your courage and do the unthinkable: Send him off to school with a lunch box containing only a sandwich and a carton of yogurt—sans spoon. I can promise you that come Wednesday morning, his lunch box will be prepared.

Of course, it's important to lay the ground rules with your children before you let them experience any unpleasant consequences of their forgetfulness. Let them know ahead of time that you will not be picking up the slack if they neglect to fulfill their responsibility. I've warned Kaitlyn, for example, that if she doesn't clean out her lunch box on any given afternoon, neither will I, and at lunchtime she'll open her lunch to discover yesterday's debris alongside today's cuisine.

Hard-line? Sure. But, who knows? Maybe if our kids can learn something about the relationship between actions and consequences over something as trivial as a school lunch, they won't have to learn this lesson from scratch as a teenager or adult, when the issues are more serious and the stakes much higher!

Kids and food. What a partnership! Hopefully it's a relationship that can produce more than full tummies and strong bones . . . hopefully it can create some good family memories as well. If you want happy meals with your kids (and I'm not talking McDonald's here), then consider some of the suggestions in this chapter. And when it comes to all the food issues I didn't have a chance to examine, well, just keep watching Robert Stack. Sooner or later he'll do a program on something really helpful:

Like how many fingers does a chicken have anyway?

### Restaurant Survival Techniques for Parents of Small Children

- *Time* your excursions so they are compatible with your child's needs and schedule.
- Have realistic *expectations* regarding your child's behavior.
- Maintain a positive *attitude.*
- *Prepare* ahead of time as much as you can. Ideas include packing snacks, books, quiet toys . . . even making menu decisions before you get to the restaurant.
- Be willing to help *entertain* your little ones before their food arrives.
- Select a dining *environment* that is child-friendly.

## Myth #3

# You Can't Take It with You

 have a dream. I would love to spend a month traveling around Europe toting only a backpack. This would be in sharp contrast to the way I have to travel now, which is with a packhorse. This is because I am a parent, and traveling with a family often requires mass quantities of paraphernalia and sometimes even support staff.

You and I have always heard that "you can't take it with you." It's obvious that whoever said this never traveled with small children.

With a baby in the house, it seems as though I have to pack a suitcase just to walk out my front door. Last week was the worst: I spent forty-five minutes packing diapers, snacks, toys, pacifiers, baby wipes, juice, and blankets, and hauled it all outside only to find out that the mail hadn't even come yet.

## Accessorizing Your New Baby

It's so misleading when you give birth. Your baby comes into the world with nothing but a smile and you look at him and think there's nothing as pure and simple as an infant. Of course, what you don't know is that there is *nothing* simple about it. You soon learn that babies require all sorts of special equipment, doodads, and accessories. They don't come with all the stuff they need because a fully equipped baby would never fit through a birth canal, but that doesn't mean you can skimp on buying all these things once they are actually here.

What I don't understand is why babies keep getting more complicated. A hundred years ago babies required a lot less accessorizing. In some eras all you needed was a wet nurse (which as an accessory eats more than, say, a stroller, but is far more versatile).

Even the last decade has seen a surge in complexity regarding babies. Eight years slipped by between the birth of my first and second babies, and I have been amazed to discover how much more sophisticated baby-rearing has become in that length of time. With my first baby, for example, I monitored the temperature of bathwater with my wrist (silly me!). Today, for around twenty bucks I can buy a bath mat on which the words "Too Hot" appear in bubbles coming out of the mouth of a hippopotamus.

There are lots of other innovations, too. When I was a baby I had a plain old teddy bear. Ten years ago, Kaitlyn had a teddy bear that played a melody. Today I can buy Kacie a bear that, when you push a button, makes womb noises. (My only question—besides what a "womb noise" sounds like—is whether the womb sounds are loud enough to be heard over the musical pacifier. It plays "Twinkle Twinkle Little Star" at the first hint of suction.)

Other innovations center around food and feeding. For example, there's a long-sleeved bib on the market . . . a booster

41

*You soon learn that babies require all sorts of special equipment, doodads, and accessories. They don't come with all the stuff they need because a fully equipped baby would never fit through a birth canal, but that doesn't mean you can skimp on buying all these things once they are actually here.*

seat that collapses and fits in your dishwasher . . . and even a bottle warmer that plugs into the cigarette lighter in your car.

Still, of all the new products on the market, few can compete with the battery-operated vibrating teething ring. (Except maybe the "tinkle targets" you drop in the commode to help your toddler learn how to take aim in life.)

In case you are wondering if I'm making these up, let me assure you that I am not. These are actual products. The fact that there are items on the market like vibrating teething rings seems to suggest two things—the first being that some employees have too much time on their hands, and the second being that if families are buying these items, there's no telling what else they might buy. This means there are still plenty of opportunities for innovative thinkers to further complicate our lives as parents. Many other creative products are, in fact, just begging to be invented, walkers with airbags and glow-in-the-dark potties among them.

## Needs versus Wants

How much of this stuff do we really need? The answer is different for every family.

My tendency is to think I "need" anything that can be acquired via a really good sale. I've always suspected a kindred spirit whenever I hear the joke about the woman who came home from the supermarket and asked her husband to help her unload three cases of dog food from her trunk. When he reminded her they didn't own a dog, she said, "I know, but I saved 40 percent!"

Last fall I came home from the store with four inflatable pool toys that had each been marked down from twelve dollars to three. (If you're tracking with me, I probably don't need to tell you that we don't have a pool.) Then, I recently went to a garage sale and bought a brand-new infant carrier for a buck, despite the fact that my husband assures me our child-bearing years are over. Furthermore, three years ago a local supermarket ran a REALLY good special on barbecue sauce. I bought fifteen bottles, three of which are still in my pantry (I guess even in Texas you can consume just so much barbecue). I opened a bottle two days ago and discovered an alternative fuel source that NASA should be pretty excited to hear about.

My point is that no one can accuse me of talking out of turn when I say that, if we're not careful, we can end up buying things we don't really need.

So what are the necessary accessories that families REALLY can't do without? If musical pacifiers and tinkle targets aren't on the list, what is?

## Indispensable Resources for Savvy Parents

I spoke with some moms and dads and asked them to name one indispensable resource that has helped them be a better parent. Okay, a few parents cheated and gave me two things, but most of them played by the rules. I found much of what they had to say thought-provoking, their words challenging me toward greater heights in my own role as a parent. My hope is that their insights will inspire you as much as they did me.

### *The Wisdom of Ages*

"Name one resource? Grandparents. They really have the ability and the time to instill values and self-esteem in the children. They're more patient than we are, for one thing. Sometimes they're more creative too: My mother-in-law has a lot to offer in that department, like having my kids say the ABCs while they wash their hands, to make sure they wash long enough to do some good. Even magic tricks. Who has time to bother with magic tricks, other than a grandparent?

"My husband and I also appreciate the advice we receive. Our parents have experienced a lot of life and see the bigger picture. When they come to visit, sometimes they'll say things like, 'You're too hard on this kid,' or, 'That one's really pushing your buttons; have you considered . . . ?' We don't feel like they're meddling because we know they want the best for us and for our kids.

"I read an article recently in the magazine *Modern Maturity*. The author said that he goes to retirement homes and tells the folks there to quit playing shuffleboard and go spend time with their grandkids. I couldn't agree more! Retirement has become about 'self,' but it should be about reaching out and sharing what you have learned with others. Grandparents have so much to give, and families today desperately need what they have to offer."

Jackie, mother of three
ages 2, 7, and 10

### That's the Book for Me

"The Bible has been an invaluable resource for me. It proves itself over and over again. For one thing, as I read the Bible I am reminded how I need to develop my own character, which gives me insights into how to develop the character of my children. It also inspires me by giving me the history of people who have lived before me, people whose characters were changed and molded by God. One example is David. He committed some of the worst sins, sleeping with another man's wife and then arranging for her husband to be killed. And yet he went from that tragic point in his life to writing the Psalms and being described as having a heart for God. If God could forgive David, helping him become a true man of God, then I know that I can be forgiven of anything and so can my child."

Christi, mother of one

age 10

### Consistency in the Heat of Battle

"My two younger children are really stubborn and can really pitch a fit. Sometimes it seems easier to walk away and not deal with it, but then I remember that they're wrong, and I'm right, and that I can't let them win this battle. It's hard to be consistent day in and day out, but it's important for their development.

"Of course, you have to be careful not to win for winning's sake if you see that it's going to cause more harm than good. You don't want to break a child's spirit in the process. I think the key is to choose your battles, and then make sure that you prevail. Determine which battles will have the greatest impact on your child's character. Forget the fight over which color socks to wear, and focus on the battles that are about who is going to be in charge."

Darla, mother of three

ages 6, 10, and 12

### It's Not What You Know but Who You Know

"Relationships. It's all about relationships, and the first and most important is the father's relationship with the Lord. Then comes the relationship between husband and wife and the relationship that they share together with God. From these foundational relationships spring the resources you need to raise your children. When things are right between God and me and between my wife and me, and together we are right with our Creator, then and only then will we be equipped to be effective parents."

Ed, father of five
ages 10 to 27

## Support Networks Make Good Sense

"For starters, my mother has been an indispensable resource. Her advice and counseling mean a lot. I could say the same thing about my friends and the advice and support I get from them.

*"If God could forgive David, helping him become a true man of God, then I know that I can be forgiven of anything and so can my child."*

"Sometimes you think you're the only one dealing with a problem. Then, in everyday conversation with friends, things will emerge that help you to understand that you're not the oddball, that everyone deals with these things. You discover, for example, that yours isn't the only daughter who loses her temper and stomps off and slams the door to her room. You can get such encouragement and hope, particularly from other parents who have made it through tough times and survived."

Deemie, mother of one
age 12

## Role Models Set the Pace

"I realize that not everyone receives good role modeling from their own parents. And yet a positive role model can and should be a major resource. In my case, my parents did a lot of good things, and there were some things they didn't do. In terms of teaching us morality and doing things with us, they were great examples. There wasn't much focus, however, on intimate communication or spiritual principles.

"Look at the things your parents did right and then, if there are any gaps, look for other examples to give you guidance. In my life, I filled in the gaps by studying the Scriptures and also through relationships with godly men willing to relate their own experiences as husbands and fathers. I meet once a week, for example, with a man from church who has been honest in talking about his own family, things he did right and things he would do differently if he had the chance.

"There's a biblical injunction for older women to teach the younger women. I think it's important for men and women both to have these kinds of relationships. My heart is heavy over the fact that churches haven't done as good a job as they should have in encouraging mentoring relationships of this caliber. Pastor Howard Hendricks says that men need three types of other men in their lives: a 'Paul,' an older man who can be a godly example; a 'Barnabas,' a peer with whom they can be accountable; and a 'Timothy,' someone younger to guide and disciple. We're missing that in the church today."

Mike, father of three<br>ages 6, 10, and 12

## Life Is a Journey—Whatcha Gonna Pack?

Now ask yourself a question. What about you? What is the one resource that has helped you in your efforts to be the best parent you can be? How can you use that resource more effectively? Are there other resources available to you that you haven't maximized? Can you use any of the ideas from our panel of parents quoted in the paragraphs above?

Parenting is a tough job. When we're looking for helpful aids, one option is to go to Target and stroll the children's department. An even better idea might be to consider intangible resources, searching our own hearts, seeking spiritual guidance, mining our relationships with parents and spouses and friends and mentors.

Life as you and I know it on Planet Earth appears to require the possession and management of lots of "things." As we journey through life, we have a tendency to haul our possessions with us, whether we're talking about strollers and port-a-cribs, or furniture and cars and all the other trappings of comfortable living in the '90s.

We take it all with us, don't we?

Of course, in the very end, as we leave this life and journey into eternity, some things get left behind, musical pacifiers and tinkle targets among them.

But we hardly go empty-handed. Our bags are packed for that journey as well, filled with the things that rust and decay can't touch:

Memories of our years raising our families . . .

The impact of the quality of our relationships with our spouses, parents, children, and others . . .

The love we feel for our kids and their love for us . . .

And, hopefully, the joy that comes from knowing we loved hard and laughed long and lived with passion, integrity, and fire.

In this life—and on into the next—no one travels empty-handed. We take something with us. Let's choose wisely!

 ## Trends in Baby Paraphernalia

As if we don't own enough stuff already, here are some products that are just begging to be invented. To my knowledge, these products don't yet exist, but probably should:

*Glow-in-the-dark potty seats* for when your toddler needs to go to the bathroom in the middle of the night. Come to think of it, a husband-sized version might not be a bad idea either.

*Walkers with air bags.*

The *combination pacifier/beeper.* A "must have" for those moments when your baby is screaming at the top of her lungs and you've got about fifteen seconds to find the pacifier before the neighbors call the police. Just go to any phone, dial a phone number, and the pacifier will beep until located.

*Strollers with cup- and bottleholders.* I'd be willing to pass on the leather seat, CD player, and surround sound. But the cupholder is a must.

*Baby-proof shoes* that are not adult-proof as well. Baby shoes with Velcro work fine for a few months but then they cease being footwear and become dexterity toys as your baby discovers that he can remove them faster than you can say, "Jared, stop playing with that shoe."

Shoelaces can be double-tied to deter even the most ambitious baby, but they also serve double duty as idiot-tests for moms and dads who can't untie them either. Shoes with miniature padlocks might work if parents could be trusted not to lose the keys. All things considered, shoes with combination locks are probably our best bet. But let's make the combination easy to remember. Something simple, but not simple enough for our kids to figure out. It's got to be something that parents know about, but kids don't. I'd suggest using the code word "sex," but parents of small children might not remember what it is, much less how to spell it.

Maybe Velcro isn't such a bad idea after all.

# Better Late Than Never

W here is it written that every married couple must consist of one person for whom timeliness is next to godliness and another person who thinks time is a weekly newsmagazine?

In my family, I'm the one who believes that time is relative, watches aren't necessarily meant to be watched, and deadlines are merely suggestions. Last week I was coordinating a get-together with another couple when the husband inquired, "You said meet at six? Do you mean Karen-time or real time?"

"Early" is not a word that frequents my vocabulary. Even early morning is a concept that is incompatible with my lifestyle. Once I had to get up at 5:00 A.M. to meet someone at the airport, and I borrowed Larry's alarm clock to wake me up. I figured that *my* alarm clock had never been exposed to such an uncivilized hour and I saw no reason to break a perfectly good tradition.

Larry, on the other hand, likes to arrive early to everything. His wristwatch, car clock, and office clock are all set five minutes fast. We argue about promptness all the time. I know it's hard to believe, but he would actually prefer to skip church and stay home altogether rather than walk into a service forty minutes late.

## When Opposites Attract

They say that opposites attract, which appears to be true. But they never tell you the whole story, which is that opposites can also annoy. This is often the result when two people marry and move in together despite the fact that their internal clocks are running on completely different time zones.

Maybe that's my problem. Born and raised in Southern California, I'm still functioning in the Pacific time zone while my husband—a native Hoosier—is rooted in central. No wonder I'm still sleeping at 9:00 when we're supposed to be walking out the door to go to church—it feels like 7:00 A.M. to me.

I guess we could pass a law prohibiting people from marrying across state lines. But even that measure wouldn't help those of us who are already struggling with interzonal marriages.

Not to mention those of us who have interzonal marriages *and* have children.

There's something almost heroic about trying to get out the door—on time—with children, particularly small ones. Sometimes I think it poses the kind of epic challenge that is of similar caliber to, say, scaling Mount Everest with one hand tied behind your back: Your chances of success are nil, but there is something poignant and even noble about trying it anyway.

They say "better late than never." But the truth is that, in some households, if you're running late, tensions can run so high that it's better to cut your losses and just stay home.

51

So, what are our alternatives? How can we ease the process of getting from here to there? What steps can we take to diffuse conflict between those who are prompt and those of us who have yet to hear the national anthem sung at a ballgame, who have never seen the previews at the movie theater, and who feel that the words "first come, first served" are discriminatory and should be struck from the English language?

## Procrastinators Unite

I'd love to start a support group for people who have a hard time arriving anywhere on time. The meetings would convene sometime between 7:00 P.M. and the closing prayer. I've been intending to place an announcement about the group in the classifieds, but somehow I keep missing the newspaper deadline.

> They say "better late than never." But the truth is that, in some households, if you're running late, tensions can run so high that it's better to cut your losses and just stay home.

The other thing I'm struggling with is a good name for such a group. Latecomers Anonymous doesn't quite work. In fact, using the word "anonymous" at all would be a misnomer. This is because it's often difficult for late people to keep a low profile. Anonymity does not come easy when you're slithering twenty minutes late into an auditorium filled with four hundred people who conspired together to make sure that the last empty seat in the building is located in the front row.

Despite the challenges, I still think it would help if individuals who struggle with tardiness could get together and talk about the problem. Wouldn't it be great to exchange ideas, insights, and solutions? I mean *real* solutions. None of this "set your watch five minutes faster" routine. Anyone who has tried this knows that your brain quickly learns to make the adjustment. In fact, with enough practice you can easily look at any timepiece anywhere in the world and give yourself an extra five minutes just in case that clock happens to be fast.

One of the really helpful things that members of a support group could work on would be apology etiquette. Assuming that you know what it's like to run behind schedule, let me ask you a question: Don't you get tired of coming up with excuses and apologies for arriving late? Sometimes, when you're REALLY late, don't you wish something drastic would happen—like running out of gas or getting mugged—so you would have a really good reason for being tardy?

In light of the chronically tardy person's unending need for fresh excuses, let's look at some common apology strategies.

One option is to throw out a vague disclaimer such as, "You wouldn't believe my morning . . ." and hope that everyone assumes that your house burned to the ground or that you were hijacked by terrorists on the way to work, without your having to actually verbalize these things.

Another option, as you greet your party, is to describe an actual event, such as the fact that your cat got his tail lodged in his throat and you had to rush him to the vet. You don't necessarily have to disclose that this occurred last summer.

If you have a serious case of chronic tardiness, you might even find yourself practicing excuses that you will probably never need. This usually occurs in the context of speeding down the freeway and rehearsing things to say to a police officer just in case you are pulled over and need to dissuade him from slapping you with a two-hundred-dollar fine.

Okay, so maybe the agenda for the support group needs a little work. But you have to admit that the idea of networking in search of road-tested solutions isn't a bad one.

## Coping with Time-Related Trauma

I contacted some chronically tardy friends—and a few early bird spouses as well—and asked for their help. What I wanted to know was this: Could they suggest any firsthand insights that might make life easier for the family in which both early birds and late bloomers reside?

And the results are in. Here are a handful of strategies and suggestions for families tired of time-related traumas.

*Don't you get tired of coming up with excuses and apologies for arriving late? One option, as you greet your party, is to describe an actual event, such as the fact that your cat got his tail lodged in his throat and you had to rush him to the vet. You don't necessarily have to disclose that this occurred last summer.*

### Ponder

Before the next crisis arises and you find yourself racing out the door with your shoes in one hand and mascara in the other, take a few moments to ask yourself a couple questions. In pondering your philosophies about promptness, you just might gain some insights into how to better tame your tardy tendencies.

Begin by asking yourself: "Is there something about arriving early that I don't like?" Sometimes it's difficult to identify why, over and over again, events seem to conspire to keep us from hitting a time target. And yet, perhaps the mystery isn't so ironclad after all. For some of us, the idea of arriving early is accompanied by a host of subtle anxieties, insecurities, and complexities. Maybe we don't enjoy those unstructured, awkward moments before everyone arrives and a social event shapes into something recognizable. Perhaps there's something unsettling about being the second person to arrive at the office, unfamiliarly quiet before coworkers show up and stress and adrenaline kick in.

The flip side of the coin is to consider the possibility that we are deriving some intangible benefit from being late. My dad tells the story of driving to a meeting with a friend who is chronically late to every conceivable event. They were actually making good time and were destined to arrive *on time* when my dad's friend pulled his car into the parking lot of a local restaurant, insisting that they grab a quick cup of coffee. As a result, they arrived late to the meeting. Until then, my dad never suspected that his friend's tardiness was intentional, nor that the grand entrances he was prone to make were anything but circumstantial.

Are we benefiting in any way from perpetual tardiness? By avoiding early arrivals, is there some gain that we are enjoying? Until we recognize the quiet motivations that are driving our behavior, we may find that permanent change is difficult to master.

## *Prepare*

Preparing in advance for timely transitions between places or events is one of the most effective things we can do to beat the clock. Here are some examples:

One mom told me that every Saturday night she lays out her kids' church clothes and packs the baby's diaper bag.

Knowing that he had to catch an early Wednesday morning flight, Larry made a special trip the night before to put gas in the car.

One woman I know prepares for hectic school mornings by setting the breakfast table before she goes to bed at night.

Some people are better at this sort of thing than others. Luckily, this is the kind of skill that, if it doesn't come instinctually, can certainly be learned. The bad news is that learning a new skill takes time and commitment; the good news is that creatures of all brain sizes are capable of learning new skills. This is how chickens learn to play the piano, horses learn how to do math, and monkeys train scientists to let them wear britches, sleep in real beds, and play with alphabet blocks all day long. Even my golden retriever is trainable. It took months, but I finally trained Misty Penny never to urinate on the living room carpet until I leave the room.

I've been trying to train myself to plan ahead. I began by making a list of all the mishaps and confusions that seem to occur as I'm trying to get out the front door. My goal is to analyze each item on the list and see if it can't be overcome by prior planning. One thing that always seems to set me back is looking for matching earrings. It seems as though I'm always misplacing one of a pair. Just after Christmas I lost the mate to one of my favorite earrings. Then as I was taking ornaments off the Christmas tree a week later, lo and behold, guess what I found hanging on a pine branch between a plastic icicle and a ceramic gingerbread man? You guessed it. My earring.

How can I redeem the time I waste cruising the house looking for wayward earrings? Well, I've got a couple ideas, one of which is to coordinate my closet in such a way that attached to every hanger is a plastic baggie holding the appropriate jewelry for that outfit. Another is to buy a tackle box with lots of little compartments and keep my earrings organized there. Or I might buy extra pairs of favorite earrings so my odds of finding a match improve. I guess I could also line up my earring choices the night before a big event so I'm not caught scrounging at the last minute.

My point is that there are probably a dozen solutions to my problem (some more realistic than others). With some forethought and planning, I just might reduce the time I spend in frenetic last-minute searching.

What can you do ahead of time to make leave-taking simpler? How about making school lunches at night? Stocking your car with spare diapers and wipes? Keeping a summer pool bag ready-to-go with swimsuits, sunscreen, visors, and towels? Reorganizing your coat closet? Making a spare set of house and car keys?

Prepare now.

Reap the benefits later.

### Leave a Margin for Emergencies

Oh, this is a tough one for me. If it takes half an hour to drive somewhere, my early-bird friends allow themselves forty minutes. I allow myself nine and hope all the lights are green.

How can I retrain myself to make better use of time margins? How can you? Let's start by listing some of the possible reasons we don't leave ourselves any margins now.

1. We have too many things to do and not enough time to do them.
2. We don't want to arrive anyplace too soon because waiting around would be a waste of time.
3. We lost too many brain cells while breast-feeding and now have no sense of time.
4. We don't own wristwatches, and all the clocks in our homes are set at slightly different times so we never actually know what time it really is anyway.
5. We've been late to so many things so many times that it's hard to visualize ourselves making different choices.
6. We're optimists who always believe a spare moment exists to do ONE LAST THING as long as we move very, very fast.

7. We manage our lives by crisis anyway and, since ideas are relative, the concept of "emergency" has become moot.

If none of these reasons make sense to you, you're probably an early bird. If a few of them make sense, you probably struggle with tardiness, but the good news is that you're teachable. If you can relate to every single item on the above list, then you and I are kindred spirits. I'd say let's get together for lunch but we'd probably have a hard time arriving at the same restaurant on the same day.

Okay. Let's look at the list again. This time let's see if we can come up with some healthier responses. Ready? Begin.

*1. We have too many things to do and not enough time to do them.* Do you know what will help us out in this area? PLANNING! Reread the previous section on preparation. Make your own list of last-minute things that tend to sabotage your efforts at promptness, and then see how you can neutralize the saboteurs ahead of time. Do you know what else will help? DON'T OVERCOMMIT. An overcommitted schedule is a written guarantee that your life will be filled with too many things to do and not enough time to do them. We'll be talking about overcommitment in the next section.

*2. We don't want to arrive anyplace too soon because waiting around would be a waste of time.* The reality is that you and I probably waste far more time scurrying around unproductively, rushing out the door without directions and getting lost, or sitting by the side of the road while some guy wearing a badge gives us his autograph. The truth is that there's nothing wasteful about arriving somewhere calm and cool with a few minutes to spare to collect our thoughts. And if I still haven't convinced you, arrive early anyway—just bring along a book or some stationery or your bank statement for something productive to do in those few spare moments.

*3. We lost too many brain cells while breast-feeding and now have no sense of time.* The good news is that the brain is a complex organism, and it can learn to compensate for those missing brain cells. This is another way of saying that this is a lousy excuse and we just have to buck up and try harder.

*4. We don't own wristwatches, and all the clocks in our homes are set at slightly different times so we never actually know what time it really is anyway.* I know you think that I made this up, and I wish you were right. Unfortunately, this example comes from my life. Just this morning I was on the phone with a friend when I asked him what time it was. Dave said, "8:30. Why?"

I told him, "Because the clock right in front of my face says 7:45, and the clock in the living room says 11:30, so I wasn't sure."

I'll be the first to admit that having your clocks vary by nearly four hours is ridiculous. Most days the clocks in my house vary within an hour and a half of each other, which I think is a more reasonable gap, especially when you consider that one hour can usually be attributed to daylight savings time since I never manage to get around to changing all of my clocks at the same time.

But I'm trying to do better. A couple months ago I bought a watch. This helps immensely. It'll help even more when I buy the batteries to go in it.

*5. We've been late to so many things so many times that it's hard to visualize ourselves making different choices.* If we have been late bloomers for a very long time, we may not be able to begin to imagine that life can be any different. Our expectations for ourselves may have conformed themselves to our past behavior, pretty much sealing our fate in the future.

We can begin today, however, to create new expectations and new "mind maps" for ourselves. Our imaginations are powerful resources. This is good. It's biblical. Our imaginations are gifts from our Creator, and he's pleased when we use them wisely.

To do this, take several minutes this evening and think about the next time you will be required to be someplace—

*I'll be the first to admit that having your clocks vary by nearly four hours is ridiculous. Most days the clocks in my house vary within an hour and a half of each other, which I think is a more reasonable gap, especially when you consider that one hour can usually be attributed to daylight savings time since I never manage to change all of my clocks at the same time.*

maybe work or church or school—at a given time. Now think about how you usually leave the house when you're behind schedule—flustered and stressed. Next, mentally stamp a big red circle and slash on that picture. (You know what I'm talking about—remember the Ghostbusters symbol or no-smoking sign?) Finally—in your mind's eye—picture yourself leaving the house calm and collected and AHEAD OF SCHEDULE. Dwell on this image for several minutes. Imagine it vividly and with great detail. How are you dressed? What are you carrying in your hands? What did you do to streamline your leave-taking? When you get to your destination, what do you do? How does it feel to be so collected and in control?

Practice this exercise frequently—even daily—for several weeks. During this time, make small efforts to model your real-life behavior after the behavior in your mind. You may be surprised at how easily the changes occur. This is because practicing in your imagination gives you a new "mind map" to follow. Suddenly the actions aren't so difficult for your body to follow—in fact, they are familiar patterns, thanks to the power of your imagination.

6. *We're optimists who always believe a spare moment exists to do ONE LAST THING as long as we move very, very fast.* What can we possibly be thinking? For optimists and pessimists alike, with every deadline comes a time when all the sand is gone . . .

the alarm is sounding . . . the count-down has reached "Zero . . . Blastoff!" This means it's time to leave. Vamoose. Scram. Skedaddle even.

The only time that there is *always* a spare moment to squeeze in one last thing is when we really don't care whether or not we get to our destination on time, or maybe even whether we get there at all. If arrival—and particularly prompt arrival—is a priority, then there comes a time when there are no spare minutes left. Don't wash that last break-fast dish . . . or put in that load of laun-dry before you head out the door . . . or go back upstairs for that letter you for-got to mail yesterday . . . or answer that ringing phone . . . unless you make the conscious choice that the dish, laundry, letter, or phone is a higher priority than getting to your destination on time.

The key word is *focus*. When you're running late and your heart is pound-ing and adrenaline is coursing through your body, your mind also revs up to a higher pitch. It's easy in this state to be-come distracted by 101 legitimate but nonessential things that need to be done. Ask yourself, "Can this wait until later?" If so, then forget about it. Focus on getting out the door. Everything else will still be there for you when you get back home.

*When you're running late and your heart is pounding and adrenaline is coursing through your body, your mind also revs up to a higher pitch. It's easy to become distracted by 101 legitimate but nonessential things that need to be done. Instead, focus on getting out the door. Everything else will still be there for you when you get back home.*

7. *We manage our lives by crisis anyway and, since ideas are relative, the concept of "emergency" has become moot.* Does the tyranny of the urgent rule your life? Are your days

spent reacting to crises around you? If so, leaving a margin of time for any emergencies might seem pointless since your whole life feels like one big emergency. If this is the case, it might be time to think about a major overhaul. Do you need to change jobs? Volunteer less at church? Streamline your kids' four thousand activities? Hire some domestic help? If your life is overbooked and careening crazily out of balance, getting out the door on time may be the least of your worries. Work on the big picture. Later you can come back and iron out details like how to arrive at Sunday school before all the donuts are taken.

### *Don't Overcommit*

This has been covered to some extent in previous paragraphs, so I won't take a lot of time here. But let me just say that part of good time management is saying no. If you pack your day too tightly, you're going to run behind schedule. It's as simple as that. Do you have a hard time saying no when people ask you to add yet another project, event, or commitment to your busy life? Here are ten ways to say "Thanks, but no thanks":

"I'd love to, but this isn't a good time for me to make that kind of commitment."

"My plate's pretty full at the moment; I'm going to have to say no."

"Not this time."

"I'm going to have to pass."

"I can't be involved at this time. But let me make a recommendation of someone else who might be willing to help. Have you considered asking _____?"

"I wish I could say yes, but my schedule at the moment is filled to the brim."

"It would be a mistake for me to take on that project right now because I don't have the time available to do the best job."

"Thanks, but no thanks."

"I cannot, in good conscience, make another commitment right now."

"No."

## *Watch That Clock*

Another key to success is equipping yourself with the resources you need to manage your life in a timely manner. Make sure you have reliable timepieces throughout your home. Equip your bedroom, kitchen, living areas, bathrooms, and even your car with good clocks. Invest in a reliable wristwatch too. This way, as you are getting ready to head out the door, there will be less chance of losing track of time and not being aware of the fact that you are dropping behind schedule.

## In Summary

Ponder your philosophies about promptness.

Prepare as much as you can ahead of time.

Allow a margin of time for emergencies or unexpected delays.

Don't overcommit your time.

Equip yourself with reliable timepieces.

See? It's not so complicated. I think we can do it. And on the days when we ponder and prepare and equip—and everything imaginable goes bust and we still find ourselves on the wrong side of the hour—let's not be too hard on ourselves. There's something, after all, to be said for being able to laugh at the flaws and foibles of life.

63

But if the stress-o-meter climbs even higher and the act of getting yourself or your family out the door means you'll have to unwind later by eating mass quantities of chocolate, or makes you consider doing bodily harm to any family member, pet, or household appliance, then chill out. Lock the doors, take the phone off the hook, and just stay home. If you never arrive at your destination, will you be missed? Probably. But that doesn't change the fact that sometimes being late is far scarier than just being absent. Besides, just because everybody's wrong about the "better late than never" theory doesn't mean they're wrong about everything.

Who knows? Maybe absence really does make the heart grow fonder.

 ## Ten Ways to Say NO

Is "Overcommitment" your middle name? Do you hate to turn anyone down? Do you say yes before thinking? If overcommitment is making you run behind schedule, here are ten ways to say, "Thanks, but no thanks":

1. "I'd love to, but this isn't a good time for me to make that kind of commitment."
2. "My plate's pretty full at the moment; I'm going to have to say no."
3. "Not this time."
4. "I'm going to have to pass."
5. "I can't be involved at this time. But let me make a recommendation of someone else who might be willing to help. Have you considered asking _____?"

6. "I wish I could say yes, but my schedule at the moment is filled to the brim."
7. "It would be a mistake for me to take on that project right now because I don't have the time available to do the best job."
8. "Thanks, but no thanks."
9. "I cannot, in good conscience, make another commitment right now."
10. "No."

## Myth #5

# Love Means Never Having to Say You're Sorry

emember the movie *Love Story?* Remember the poignant observation made by Ali McGraw's character as she neared the end of her short life and shorter marriage? It became a pop-culture staple (and a gold mine for companies peddling stickers, keychains, and plastic figurines).

You know what the phrase was. Come on. Let's say it together: "Love means never having to say you're sorry."

I'd like to know what lobotomy alumnus came up with this line.

Now, before you think I'm being too harsh, hear me out: If you love someone, you make an effort to have your lives overlap as much as possible. You share things like time, heart-to-heart conversation, responsibilities, goals, the bathroom sink, even the checkbook.

And the bottom line is that you cannot share a bathroom sink or checkbook with someone without the need arising for a good solid apology now and then.

They say that familiarity breeds contempt. Personally, I think that contempt is too strong of a word. I do believe, however, that familiarity can fuel frustration. And when frustration bites, the words "I'm sorry" are about as potent an antidote as you can find on the market.

*Are the words enough, or does a kid really need to feel sorry in order to execute a successful apology?*

The fact is that, despite pop-culture philosophy, a sincere apology is as crucial to family life as, say, toilet paper or the microwave. Unfortunately, the words "I'm sorry" are among the most underused in our vocabularies. In fact, if you live in a houseful of children, the only words you hear less often are probably along the lines of: "You do so much for me already. Please don't give me any allowance this month," or perhaps, "Look, Mom! I cleaned my room . . . just for fun!"

## Apology Etiquette for Children

If the words "I'm sorry" are vastly underused by family members of all ages, the words "Say you're sorry" comprise one of the more popular phrases in the vocabulary of today's parents. In fact, statistics indicate that if every parent in the United States, in alphabetical order, were given a penny for each time he or she has told an offspring to apologize, there would be an international copper crisis long before "Johnson."

How many times have you had this conversation with a child:

"Junior, that was a mean thing to do to your brother. Say you're sorry."

"Sry."

"You didn't mean it. Say it again."

Of course Junior didn't "mean it." If he'd had any intentions of feeling sorry about his actions, he wouldn't have tied his brother's shoelaces together and pushed him into that mud puddle in the first place!

Who knows? Maybe the person who needs to apologize in this situation is the parent for putting Junior through the trauma of first being forced to lie . . . and then being forced to lie *convincingly*.

Our goals as parents are admirable. It's just that our task is a tough one.

Here's the question: Are the words enough, or does a kid really need to *feel* sorry in order to execute a successful apology? And if our goal is for our kids to offer sincere apologies, how can we help them do it?

Let me tell you a little success story. It took place in my house last month and provided one of those shining moments when you nod your head and smile and enjoy a warm-fuzzy and think to yourself how lucky you are to be a parent. I just wish I could take some of the credit. But actually, the architect of the event was my friend Cherie Spurlock.

Cherie and her family live next door. They are practically family . . . adopted relatives . . . in-laws in love. So it's no surprise that our daughters, both ten, sometimes quarrel more like siblings than friends.

We experienced one of those moments last month over a homemade toy. By the time it was over, both girls were mad and hurt. I tried the ol' "Say you're sorry" routine but the wounds were too fresh, and pride and anger got in the way.

I was at a loss to know what to do. I figured the girls needed some time apart. Maybe they would be ready to apologize tomorrow. Then again, would I remember to pursue the matter?

Luckily Cherie knew what to do. She plopped both girls down in the living room and began, gently, to talk. She talked about the value of friendship and the need to resolve conflicts and about sharing and anger and pride. Were the girls listening? I think so. But as important as the content of Cherie's words was the mere presence of them. Her voice gave the girls some time to cool down, to distance themselves from the heat of the battle. In that ten or fifteen minutes, adrenaline levels dropped, jaws unclenched, hearts softened. Cherie even threw in some humor, and the girls had to work hard not to smile.

At the very end, Laura apologized, but Kaitlyn held out until Cherie and Laura were at the front door. That's when Kaitlyn grabbed Laura's hand and whisked her back into the living room, away from the ears and eyes of mothers. Of course I craned my neck around the corner and stood there long enough to witness Kaitlyn holding Laura's hands and saying earnestly, "I'm *really* sorry I was rude and . . ."

I drew back, leaving the girls to mend their friendship in private. I felt proud and grateful and, above all, humbled by the experience.

What made it work? What made this experience a "success"? I've pondered the sequence of events, and here are a few thoughts:

*Time helps.* One Fourth of July, I told Kaitlyn to go to her room over some now-forgotten infraction and not come out until she could apologize and really mean it. What changed her heart and brought her out of her room? Probably the aroma of Thanksgiving turkey in the oven.

Just kidding. But the fact remains that, while we may not want to wait actual months between transgression and repentance, sometimes the passage of time can soften a child's heart. It's possible that, after a heated conflict, it might take five minutes . . . fifteen minutes . . . even an hour before hot heads and fiery hearts can cool enough for rea-

69

son to bloom amongst the ashes. In the situation between Kaitlyn and Laura, perhaps I tried to evoke apologies too soon. Cherie's gentle lecture allowed time for the *process* of apology. If my approach had been successful (which it wasn't) I would have gotten merely words. Cherie's approach encouraged new attitudes.

*Don't let apologies slide.* I appreciate Cherie's commitment to helping our daughters work through their anger at the time of the squabble. How easy it would have been to shake our heads, throw up our hands, and let the girls part company wounded and mad.

Walking kids through the *process* of realigning the attitude of their hearts takes time. There are no magic words or quick fixes. It requires an expenditure of minutes and even hours that busy parents might be reluctant to give. Face it: you and I are busy. There may be times when our schedules scream at us to "let one slide." We may think we just don't have the time, this time, to help our kids wrestle with the issues until resolution is theirs. Yet the time we spend today helping our kids learn the ropes of apology can prevent heartache—both theirs and ours—tomorrow.

One of the things I hated, and appreciated, about my upbringing was that my parents were not ones to let conflict resolution wait until "mañana." Through my adolescence and teen years, there were frequent times when my attitude needed an adjustment, and my parents knew better than to put it off. My mom would call the school and let them know I wouldn't be in classes that day . . . my dad would cancel his business appointments . . . and the three of us would sit in the living room and talk, beseech, explain, vent, and implore until the walls between us dissolved in hugs and tears.

Don't allow your child to "let one slide" because you're too busy to help her through the experience. Also, don't neglect apology because the person who deserves the apology is too young or far away or unaware to appreciate the effort. Was your child rude to a toddler? Did he have a conflict with a friend who has since moved away? Did she take advantage of someone who is unaware of the situation?

Remember that the apology is for the sake of the apologizer as much as it is for the recipient. Your child needs to apologize for his or her own emotional and spiritual health.

Kaitlyn laughs at me when I make her apologize to Kacie for a snippy comment or mean facial expression. I agree with her that the benefit that Kacie will receive from an apology may be limited by her age; but the benefit Kaitlyn will derive from apologizing is priceless.

*If looks could kill, all the people Kaitlyn has apologized to so far would be dead.*

*Be specific in what you are asking your child to do.* Perhaps one of the most rewarding moments of last month's experience between Kaitlyn and Laura was a casual comment Kaitlyn made to me after Cherie and Laura had gone.

Kaitlyn said, "Oh yeah. I said all three parts of an apology."

She said it like it was no big deal, said it heading out of my kitchen on her way to her room to moon over Michael W. Smith.

"Wait a minute. Repeat that. You said what?" Outside I was pretty calm. Inside, however, I was doing the end-zone victory dance.

"You know," she said. "The three parts of an apology. I said them to Laura."

Oh, I knew all right. We'd been working on the "three parts of an apology" off and on for about a month, but I hadn't been too confident that my efforts were making any difference.

The three-part-apology concept was born one afternoon after I'd heard, one too many times, Kaitlyn's version of an apology. Any time I asked her to apologize, her words were more akin to a threatening growl than a reconciliation. She would glower and offer one clipped word: "SARie." If looks could kill, all the people Kaitlyn has apologized to so far would be dead.

I used to get frustrated until one day it dawned on me that she was giving me exactly what I was asking for: I was asking for her to say she was sorry, and she was, indeed, saying the word.

I realized that if I wanted something different, I had to change my request.

That's when I told her that a real apology has three different parts:

1. First, acknowledge how you offended the other person. (Examples might include: "I can see now that I was impatient with you," or "I'm sorry that I was rude yesterday," or "I shouldn't have lied to you.")

2. Second, make a statement about yourself. Say something about your feelings or intentions or sense of regret. ("I'm sorry I did that," or "I didn't realize I was being so harsh," or "I wish I had made a better choice.")

3. Finally, ask for forgiveness. ("Will you forgive me?")

The best apologies reflect a repentant spirit and softened heart. A kid (an adult, too, for that matter) is capable of spitting out a one-word "apology" without taming a combative attitude. It's more difficult, however, to maintain a hostile spirit through the process of thinking about—and verbalizing—a three-part apology.

*Practice what you preach.* Oh, here's the hard part. It's difficult, isn't it, to live our lives as an example to our kids? Try as we might, our expectations for our family don't always translate into consistent behavior for ourselves.

In fact, I would love to manufacture and market a T-shirt for parents that says simply: "Do as I say, not as I do."

I could sure use a shirt like that when I tell my kids to clean up after themselves . . . even though the kitchen table is still littered with the Christmas cards I was addressing four days ago.

I could wear it when I tell them to put their clothes in the hamper even as my wet towel lies crumpled on the bathroom floor. Or maybe when I ask them to make their beds every morning even though I usually get around to making mine an hour before I climb into it at night.

I would definitely have it on as I tell them to stop yelling at each other, while my voice is merely a decibel or two below that of a fire truck siren.

Or when I demand that they respect authority, while I drive twenty miles over the speed limit.

I can spend hours praising the virtues of honesty, but if my kids overhear me telling a telemarketer that neither Mr. Linamen nor Mrs. Linamen can come to the phone right now . . . I'd better be wearing the shirt.

And I definitely need to be wearing it when I tell my children to strive to be sweet and good-natured, while I am replaced, once a month, by my evil twin sister Patricia Monica Scalf (her monogram says it all).

You get the idea.

Consistently practicing what we preach is, unfortunately, virtually impossible. It's a good goal, but the likelihood of it happening ranks right up there with the odds of scientists discovering that, under certain circumstances, eating chocolate can give you a thinner waist, thicker hair, and whiter teeth. Which is precisely why, of all the characteristics we try to instill in our kids, the art of apology may be the single most important trait for us to master. As we go through life falling short of the exuberant expectations we have for ourselves, it's a powerful thing to be able to say to our families, "Oops . . . I goofed . . . Will you forgive me?"

When was the last time you apologized to your child? Or apologized to your spouse in front of your child? (If you hesitate to expose your child to the inner workings of a marriage relationship, ask yourself this question: Have your children ever seen you argue with your honey? If so, let them witness the apology, too . . . the verbal one, anyway.)

*The issue is not whether you or I or our children will make a stupid blunder in the next forty-eight hours. Of course we will. The question is whether or not we will respond to our mistakes with integrity, repentance, and restoration.*

Your willingness to apologize will do three things.

First, it can salve many of the hurts and wounds created on those rare occasions (translation: daily) when you make a mistake or fall short of perfection.

Second, it teaches your kids that everyone goofs up. Even parents. Nobody's perfect. This concept is important for a lot of reasons, one of which is simply because it's true. Why do you think that forgiveness is such a big part of many faiths, Judaism and Christianity included? Do you want your child to understand his or her need for God? Then don't let him buy into the false perception that, if he only tries hard enough, he can grasp perfection. He can't. You can't either. The issue is not whether you or I or our children will make a stupid blunder in the next forty-eight hours. Of course we will. This is a given. The question is whether or not we will respond to our mistakes with integrity, repentance, and restoration.

Third, if you practice the art of apology in your life, there is a very good chance that your children will learn by your example. When you're wrong, say you're sorry. In fact, do it right: use all three parts of an apology. Getting your children to apologize may still be a battle, but it just might be a battle you can win!

74

## Anatomy of a Healthy Apology

First, acknowledge how you offended the other person. (Examples might include: "I can see now that I was impatient with you," or "I'm sorry that I was rude yesterday," or "I shouldn't have lied to you.")

Second, make a statement about yourself. Say something about your feelings or intentions or sense of regret. ("I'm sorry I did that," or "I didn't realize I was being so harsh," or "I wish I had made a better choice.")

Finally, ask for forgiveness. ("Will you forgive me?")

## How NOT to Apologize

Apologize in any of these four ways and you just might find yourself in the midst of a new argument:

1. "I'm sorry I spent $400 at Target but I was *so* frustrated with you for ruining last week's dinner party by coming home late . . . and forgetting to call to let me know you'd be late . . . and forgetting to pick up ice and napkins on your way home from the office . . ." Rule of thumb: An apology that spends more time recounting the other person's sins than your own doesn't actually count as an apology. You do get credit, however, for finding a creative way to prolong the argument.

2. "I'm sorry if I hurt your feelings." What, you're not sure? Either you did or you didn't. If you did, apologize without the "if." If you didn't, stop groveling.

3. "I'm sorry you're angry with me." Almost as bad as saying, "I'm sorry I got caught," because it focuses more on the ramifications of your action than on your action itself. Aren't you sorry for whatever you did that was offensive?

If you are, try to focus your apology on what you did wrong. Tends to work better that way.

4. "I'm sorry I was such a jerk. How can you stand to be around me? I shouldn't be allowed to go on living. I can't believe you put up with me. Why don't you just shoot me and put me out of my misery?" Don't use your apology to turn the situation around and gain sympathy and strokes. Any apology that makes the other person feel obligated to sing your praises is more of a P. R. tool than an actual apology.

## Myth #6

# Finders, Keepers;
# Losers, Weepers

arents are losers.

Now don't get huffy. I don't mean that we wear nothing but polyester, or pick our noses in public, or believe that beer is a breakfast drink.

I mean that we're always losing things. In fact, it seems to me that being a parent is a long succession of losses and sacrifices. Since I've become a parent, for example, I've been asked to forfeit sleep, freedom, income, and more.

Several weeks ago my friend Diane complained that, since deciding to stay home with her newborn and preschoolers, she feared her intellect was turning to mush. Her exact words were, "Karen, I'm losing brain cells."

I wasn't surprised to hear this. In fact, I reassured her that this was to be expected. "Of course you're losing brain cells, Diane—what did you think breast milk was made of?"

The truth is that you can approach any gathering at which parents are present, and you will find represented a vast spectrum of losses, brain cells included. Search any parking lot where half the cars contain car seats and the rest are vans and you'll find more than the average percentage of bumper stickers that read, "Of all the things I've lost, I miss my mind the most." The vehicles that don't display this bumper sticker will probably boast something as equally inane such as "My daughter and my money go to the University of Pay and Play," or "My son is an honor student at Snob Hill Junior High and yours isn't, HA HA HA."

## Define Privacy

One of the first sacrifices that is made by any parent is privacy. In fact, privacy becomes a thing of the past from the very earliest stages of parenthood, meaning as soon as you announce your pregnancy.

I'll bet you thought that being pregnant simply meant getting ready to have a baby. Not so. Pregnancy is actually a nonverbal invitation for total strangers to demand detailed information regarding the most intimate aspects of your life. People you don't know from Adam will walk up to you and ask pointed questions about your ability to correctly implement birth control in the heat of passion ("Did you plan this pregnancy or was it a surprise?"). They'll demand to know how you intend to use your breasts ("Are you going to breast-feed?"). They may even want to know about future management of your reproductive organs ("Do you plan to have more children?").

All of this pales, however, in light of the probability that, sometime during your pregnancy, someone you've never laid eyes on before in your life will walk up to you and fondle your stomach. Without even asking. The first time this happened to me I was pregnant with my daughter Kaitlyn, standing in the supermarket checkout line, when an acne-faced teenaged boy bagging my groceries suddenly blurted, "Oh! You're going to have a baby!" and planted his left hand on my abdomen. I didn't know whether to laugh, cry, or call a lawyer. (What I *really* wanted to do was plant my right palm across his face. Without even asking.)

And it doesn't get any better. After the baby is born, privacy becomes nothing more than a fond but foggy memory from your preparenting days (kind of like sleep and sex). Regardless of the ages of your children, your offspring will view your body, all of your possessions, each of the hours in your day, and the sum total of your financial assets as belonging to them.

Nothing is sacred. Not even personal hygiene. My friend Cherie once confided, "Some days I have to go to the bathroom so bad. . . . When I finally get a minute and head down the hall, little voices follow me even then. I find myself shouting through the locked door, 'I have to go potty! Can't I have a moment to myself JUST TO GO POTTY!'"

Cherie and her husband recently decided they needed some time to themselves. They made arrangements for their three kids to spend the week with various friends, and then they began their dream vacation.

They stayed home.

This seems particularly amazing to me because Cherie's husband just happens to be an airline captain. This means they can fly practically anywhere they want in the entire world free of charge. Think of it! Hawaii, Greece, England, free! And the vacation paradise they chose was their own house—cozy, familiar . . . and EMPTY.

## You Only THINK You're in Charge

When you take the plunge and embark on the grand adventure of parenthood, you lose privacy. Do you know what else you lose?

Control.

> **During pregnancy you lose control of your bladder, your hormones, and your figure . . . and it goes downhill from there.**

It starts with the small things. During pregnancy you lose control of your bladder, your hormones, and your figure . . . and it goes downhill from there.

There are two children in my house now, and I have completely abandoned any illusions I might have once had about being in control of what goes on in my home. For one thing, I keep finding things in the strangest places. Once I found a Barbie in my refrigerator and a box of tampons under my pillow. Larry is always complaining about not being able to find the TV remote. He asked me recently if there was any way we could keep the remote from wandering all over the house. I told him there was, but that we were too late to use it: It's called birth control.

It would be nice if I could contain the anarchy to the point where people outside of my immediate family might buy into the false assumption that I am in charge and in control. This is, of course, a pipe dream.

Case in point: We had unexpected guests several months ago. When the woman asked to use the bathroom, I directed her to the cleanest of the three. When she rejoined the group, I politely inquired whether she had closed the bathroom door, explaining that open doors encouraged my eighteen-month-old to indulge in her favorite water sport—playing in the toilet.

My guest smiled. "Well, that explains it."

"Explains what?" I asked.

"Before I could go to the bathroom, I had to fish two wooden blocks and a set of car keys from the commode."

## Losers, Weepers . . .

Privacy. Control. Freedom. Even sanity.
*Especially* sanity.

We're destined to lose it all from the moment we gaze into the eyes of the small ones entrusted to our care.

Yes, we're losers. But why aren't we weepers? Oh, we cry now and then as we hover protectively over our charges, watching their mistakes and hurting for them and with them. But the tears aren't for the things we've lost in the process of being parents. Sometimes, in fact, the tears are out of gratitude for what we've gained.

It seems to me that there's something about the economy of family life that doesn't add up. My friends will tell you that I'm no math wizard (I'm not even a math apprentice). And yet even I can see that there's something funny going on when you sacrifice and give and lose on a daily basis . . . and end up with more than you had when you began.

What have I lost in my quest to raise a family? A bunch. What have I gained? Everything.

There's a story I want to tell you. It's about eight-year-olds and tooth fairies and friendships and pillow fights, and the profound privilege of being a parent lucky enough to share in it all. It's also about the economy of family life, where the daily investment of time and energy reap dividends more valuable than gold.

I wrote about the experience in my journal two years ago, and while I considered rewriting the experience for this chapter, I decided to let the story stand as it was originally written. So here it is, a peek over my shoulder and into the journal of one grateful mom:

### No Rest for the Weary
#### -or-
### Whoever Named Them "Slumber Parties" Obviously Never Had One

They're still giggling. It's nearly midnight, for crying out loud, and they're still cracking each other up with the kind of hilarious nonsensical babble in which eight-year-olds are particularly fluent.

What a night. It all began at 4:30 this afternoon when I called my friend Diane and invited her over for Campbell's soup and nachos. It seemed like a good idea at the time, since her husband and mine are together in Colorado Springs on business. And so Diane arrived, toting her three offspring. Laura from next door was already spending the evening with us, so this act of insanity brought the kid-total up to six—as in three eight-year-olds, two toddlers, and an infant. Hard to believe that was less than seven hours ago. It seems more like seven days.

> There's something about the economy of family life that doesn't add up. There's something funny going on when you sacrifice and give and lose on a daily basis . . . and end up with more than you had when you began.

Dining with six girls ages six months to eight years provided enough harrowing moments to stock a Stephen King novel—and that was before Kaitlyn invited Rachel and Laura to spend the night! As Diane left with her two littlest girls, I found myself faced with the challenge of shepherding three eight-year-olds through the rest of the evening. In the past few hours, we've survived one movie, several pillow fights, a bloody nose, and one tearful conflict borne of the politics of prepubescent girls.

Ah, listen to me. If I'm not careful, I might give you the idea that I'm actually complaining. The truth is, I'm having the time of my life. In the midst of all the chaos, I baked chocolate chip cookies. We lit a kerosene lamp, ate warm cookies dipped in cold milk, and took turns reading pages of a storybook by the glow of the flame. Stories about the friendship of "Frog and Toad" gave me a chance to remind the girls of how special their own friendships are, while a story entitled "Norman Fools the Tooth Fairy" prompted each girl to burst into animated reminiscences of baby teeth that she had lost.

Now the entire floor of the den has been turned, with quilts, into one magnificent nest, and the little ladies are feasting on half an apple and half a peanut butter sandwich each (okay, so I'm a pushover, but they said they were *starving*). We had one rough moment when Laura decided to sleep on the couch instead of the floor, and Kaitlyn—who figured if anyone got special treatment it should be *her*—responded with the fury of a woman, albeit a small woman, scorned. I pulled her aside, and we talked in the living room about the merits of being flexible, not to mention the finer points of being a good hostess, and finally I asked her to pray and ask God to help her grow more patient and cooperative and kind to her friends. It took several "takes" to get it right—and I'm not even counting the time she prayed, "And please, Lord, get Laura off the couch!" But finally there was a breakthrough as she prayed for a more gentle spirit with her friends.

So now they're giggling. It's not quite as good as the silence of slumber, particularly at this late hour, but it's a good sound anyway.

Tonight I talked to these girls—as a group and, later, to Kaitlyn alone—about the privilege of having good friends. I hope they remember these carefree, magic moments for the rest of their lives—the passion of their fights, the completeness of their reconciliations, the sweet abandon with which they approach their moments of hilarity, the satisfaction of secrets shared in whispers when the lights are out and they think I think they are well on their way toward sleep.

Do I envy them these profound privileges of girlhood? No way! You see, my kitchen may be in shambles and my hair in disarray . . . there may be cookie dough on my shirt and books and Barbies scattered throughout my beleaguered house . . . there's probably still blood in my bathroom sink—but my reward is coming. It's finally quiet, you see, and in a few moments I'm going to tiptoe into the den and gaze on the faces of my

*Tonight we talked about the privilege of having friends. What I didn't talk about was the privilege of being a mother, of playing a supporting role in the poignant and comedic drama of their lives.*

daughter and her two best friends, a slumbering jumble of blankets and braids and gangly limbs, their expressions innocent and peaceful in repose, mere babies on the verge of adolescence. Tonight we talked about the privilege of having friends. What I didn't talk about was the privilege of being a mother, of playing a supporting role in the poignant and comedic drama of their lives.

Yes, it's been a wild evening, chaotic and exhausting and, at times, seemingly out of control. But I wouldn't trade a moment for the world. One day I'll have peace and quiet. I'll have an orderly kitchen and clean bathrooms. My den won't look like a bomb went off in a quilt factory, and my pillows will never again ever be wielded as lethal weapons.

When that time comes, I'm sure I'll find some redeeming factor in my days, some greater purpose to guide my agenda, some fire and angst and hilarity to spark my hours. Right now, however, it's hard to imagine. Right now I'm counting my blessings.

 **Let's Brag a Little!**

Have your children enriched your life? Make a list of positive ways each child has changed your life. Then share items from your list, or maybe even your entire list, with your child.

Also, when talking with family and friends, don't hesitate to brag about how your child has enriched your life.

For one thing, talking about your kids in this manner nurtures positive feelings within you. It's also possible that your comment may be overheard by your child, or that the person you're talking to will tell your child what you said—and a compliment received in this roundabout way can build esteem faster than you can say "warm-fuzzy."

Need some ideas? My list regarding Kaitlyn looks like this:

Having Kaitlyn Linamen in my life has given me

- a new understanding and appreciation of the love my parents have for me
- the experience of loving someone more than myself
- a buddy to tell corny jokes with
- a new sensitivity to the beauty, vulnerability, and magic of life—I never cried at movies or touching stories before I became a mother!
- the chance to be a parent
- a level of joy and pride I never knew before
- someone to watch *Little Women* with
- a reading buddy—I think *Peter Pan* and *Alice in Wonderland* have been my favorites!

## Myth #7

# Father Knows Best

 efore I was a parent, I had no children but lots of theories about parenting. Now I have two children and no theories. But I'm sure you know what I'm talking about. It's the principle that says that the usefulness of your knowledge decreases in direct proportion to your need for useful information. (A related principle applies to beauty and money.)

Actually, the person in my household who seems to know the most about parenting is my ten-year-old daughter. Of course, she seems to know the most about everything under the sun. She will, undoubtedly, get smarter and smarter until the day she gives birth to her first child. At that point, it is virtually guaranteed that she will experience a massive knowledge deficit. Some experts suspect that this "brain-drain" is, in some mysterious fashion, related to the detachment of the placenta during childbirth. Others hypothesize that the knowledge deficit is actually triggered in the months and years following childbirth (more specifically, as a result of prolonged exposure to other adult victims of brain-drain who make a living by dressing up like seven-foot canaries and large purple herbivores cavorting across your television screen).

Whatever the reasons, suffice it to say that even though we all grew up believing that Father (and Mother) really did know best, now that we are parents ourselves we know the big secret: Moms and dads don't have a clue. They just make that stuff up about being omniscient to keep knowledgeable kids in check until they, too, become parents and experience a two-thirds drop in their IQ. *Then* they can be in charge.

## Mysteries of Parenting Explored

I've been a parent long enough to know that every morning brings with it some new challenge for which I am, at best, nominally prepared. Why can't kids come with instructions? Both of my babies came home from the hospital with one of those nasal suction devices they tried to adopt as pacifiers. Why don't doctors send babies home with something their parents can REALLY use . . . like a how-to manual?

I am constantly amazed by the number of times my kids have left me scratching my head in confusion or wonder. (And I'm not even referring to the time they put dish detergent in the shampoo bottle. That's another head-scratching story altogether.)

Do I know best? Sometimes I think I don't know squat. Among the many topics about which I haven't got a clue . . .

How serious is it when a two-year-old has a toe fetish? Several times a day, Kacie demands to have her "shoes and tocks" removed so she can inventory her feet. Is she destined to spend her adult life wearing sandals for easy access? When she's in seventh grade and has to write an essay on "Someone I Admire" will she choose Imelda Marcos? And is podi-

87

atry a good career choice for someone with a foot fetish, or does that border on the unethical?

And that's not the only mystery. What in the world does it mean when you are setting the table for company and find a hard glob of chewed gum tucked under the rim of your best china? Whose gum is it? Your teenage son's? When did he last eat on the good china, anyway? If it wasn't him, could one of your previous guests have done it? Shouldn't the dishwasher have melted the gum and whisked it away when the plate was washed? And if chewed gum is indeed impervious to scalding soapy water, then how long has it been there? Was it there when you served Christmas dinner to your in-laws, or when you entertained your husband's boss last month?

*Why don't doctors send babies home with something their parents can REALLY use . . . like a how-to manual?*

Where do all the missing socks go?

Why is meat loaf served at a friend's house more enticing to your kids than pizza served at home?

What do teenage girls do in the bathroom for three hours?

And what exactly does it mean when your ten-year-old loses a tooth at school, brings it home in a tiny plastic box, and then leaves it sitting for two months in a corner of your kitchen counter? Even as I write, my kitchen counter is adorned with an abandoned baby molar. Did Kaitlyn forget that it's there? Has she lost sleep at night wondering where she left her tooth and longing for her dollar from the tooth fairy? If so, why hasn't she mentioned it to me? Doesn't she know I would have helped her find it? What if she doesn't think her tooth is lost? What if she knows exactly where it is? What if a visit from the tooth fairy is the last thing on her mind? What if . . . what if she's growing up?

From potty-training dilemmas to disciplinary decisions to debates about dating, driving, and the decorative piercing of body parts, parenting offers a smorgasbord of challenging questions that promise to stump even the wisest of moms and dads.

Maybe Robert Young had all the answers when he was raising Princess, Kitten, and Bud. For the rest of us, parenting is a leap of faith . . . an unending series of unsolved mysteries . . . an adventure that takes us daily to our wits' end, and beyond.

## Resources for Clueless Parents

Now that we've established the fact that we've all bitten off more than we can chew, what options do we have? Are there principles and resources that can help us compensate for our flaws and shortcomings? I think so. Here are three suggestions that have proven helpful to me.

*1. Is honesty still the best policy?* There are two schools of thought regarding how a parent should deal with the annoying fact that he or she is fallible, imperfect, and prone to make an occasional lulu of a mistake.

The first school of thought says that, as a parent, you need to employ every possible resource to make your kids *think* that you have every answer. This approach requires you to convince your family that you are genetically unable to make a mistake. You must, indeed, persuade them that the only reason your opinions are not penned between Luke and John is because you were born too late to make the deadline.

My experience is that children figure it out sooner or later. By the time they are five years old . . . or nine . . . or seventeen . . . or perhaps when they become parents themselves—and *certainly* by their second year of therapy—kids come to the realization that Mom and Dad are fallible, imperfect beings.

The second school of thought recognizes this fact and suggests, respectfully, that parents cut to the chase. Honesty is the best policy. It's okay to let your children in on the fact that you don't know everything . . . that you are capable of a mis-

*From potty-training to body piercing, parenting challenges even the wisest of moms and dads. Maybe Robert Young had all the answers, but for the rest of us parenting is an adventure that takes us daily to our wits' end, and beyond.*

take now and then . . . and that you are committed to raising your family to the best of your ability, despite your glaring imperfections.

Now and again, during my years as a child and adolescent, my dad would offer a casual disclaimer. Naming the ages of my sisters and me, he would say, "You know, I've never done this either. I've never been a father to a nine-year-old, a seven-year-old, and a four-year-old before. You need to be patient with me, too." A few years later the statement might be changed to represent our ages at, say, twelve, ten, and seven or sixteen, fourteen, and eleven. You might think that his disclaimer might have made me feel insecure. Instead, it helped me see my parents in a new light, reminding me that we were, indeed, all on the same team and that even the best parents need to be on the receiving end of love, encouragement, and yes, even forgiveness.

*2. Teamwork can tame the tiger.* Another resource for clueless parents is teamwork. Ask your kids for their input regarding reward systems, responsibilities, and even ramifications.

Now, before you jump to the conclusion that your children will automatically suggest cash rewards for good behavior, cash rewards for bad behavior, and a sunrise curfew that even Count Dracula could have lived with, hear me out.

I've used this approach with Kaitlyn, particularly when we can't seem to put a given struggle to bed. There are simply times when the same issue crops up time and time again, and my efforts at discipline seem to go unheeded or, even worse, appear to provoke Kaitlyn into more anger or rebellion. These are the moments when I stop trying to convince her that I have all the answers and try a simpler approach.

Several months ago, for example, the issue at hand was Kaitlyn's penchant for talking back. When my disciplinary efforts fell flat, I asked her to help me solve the problem. I explained that God had given me the important job of training Kaitlyn to be a godly woman, and that "talking back" was a behavior that had to be dealt with in order for God's design for Kaitlyn to be fulfilled. I told her I was stumped on how to achieve this goal and asked her to help me come up with a solution.

"Mom, I don't *mean* to talk back. I just forget," Kaitlyn explained. "But then you get mad at me, and I get mad back, and pretty soon I'm talking back even more because I'm mad."

"So what do we do about it?" I asked.

*Have you ever wondered which of your parenting mistakes will end up being discussed on a psychologist's couch twenty years from now? Or worse, will be analyzed on the futuristic set of some spinoff of Jenny Jones or Geraldo?*

She thought a moment. "The first time I talk back, give me a code word. Like . . . pickle. Say 'pickle.' That'll remind me to stop doing what I'm doing."

"And what if the code word doesn't work?" (The cynic in me just had to ask.)

She shrugged. "Then you can yell at me."

Guess what? The code word works. Not every time, but often enough to make a difference. Corporate America calls this "buy in." If you want a team of people to perform at a certain level, let them help determine the rewards they'll receive if they're successful . . . and the ramifications they'll experience if they're not. Kaitlyn was much more willing to "buy into" a plan that she helped author, rather than a plan that was solely mine to begin with.

Of course, there are still issues that are better dealt with by a dictator than a committee. Sometimes, as a mom or dad, you just need to say, "I know you don't understand or agree, but ultimately your safety is my responsibility, and you're just going to have to live with my decision on this issue." In the final analysis, a family is closer to an autocracy than a democracy, and yet there's plenty of room for a hardy team effort among members.

*3. A Higher Power can save the hour.* Have you ever, at the close of a day filled with a particularly frustrating family saga, asked yourself which of your parenting mistakes will end up being discussed on a psychologist's couch twenty years from now? Or worse, will be analyzed on the futuristic set of some year-2027 spinoff of Jenny Jones or Geraldo?

Even the children of perfect parents can wander into trouble (I heard that Bud ended up dabbling in drugs and that Kitten spent years in therapy). So what does that mean for the children of imperfect parents like you and like me?

They don't have a chance.

Unless, of course, you and I know where to go for help.

There is an encouraging promise found in the Bible. It goes like this: "If any of you lacks wisdom, he should ask God, who gives generously to all without finding fault, and it will be given to him" (James 1:5).

What a relief for clueless parents everywhere! There is actually a way to get some help with the bazillions of parenting decisions that come our way each and every day.

And no one needs help with decisions more than I do. Decision making is not my forte. It took me two months to decide how to answer my husband's marriage proposal, and once, in a restaurant, the waitresses changed shifts twice before I actually placed my order.

Okay. So maybe they changed shifts once. The point is that it's easy to feel under siege with the number of decisions that have to be made in life. Whether decisions come easily to you, or whether, like me, you'd just as soon empty the lint trap on your dryer, the sheer quantity of decisions you face as a parent may well leave you feeling overwhelmed.

Wise up. There is a source, a Higher Power, a Person who has all wisdom and wants to help you become all that you can be as a parent, and as an individual too. You can be a wiser parent . . . and all you have to do is practice the three Rs. What are they?

> **Reading.** Check out your Bible. There is an entire book devoted to the sayings of the wisest king who ever lived. Entitled *Proverbs,* it is truly a textbook for living wisely. Read it to yourself . . . to your spouse . . . to your children. The principles in these pages can help guide you through many of life's crossroads. Whether or not you consider yourself a "Christian," you will benefit from reading and applying the wisdom in these pages.
>
> **Requesting.** Remember the verse from James? Let me paraphrase: "If you are a clueless parent who lacks wisdom, ask God." Pray about the decisions you're facing today. Mention them specifically. Then pray for your skills as a parent. Ask God to give you wisdom as you face the challenges of raising your children and being a godly partner for your spouse.
>
> **Relationship.** How well do you know the Person who gave King Solomon the wisdom you're reading about in the Bible? How well do you know the Person you are approaching in prayer? Your *reading* and your *requests* will have the greatest impact when they take place in the context of a close, personal *relationship* with God.

In the twenty-third book of the Bible, a man named Isaiah described God as "the sure foundation for your times, a rich store of salvation and wisdom and knowledge" (Isa. 33:6).

Was he talking about God as a nebulous resource? A vague higher power? A distant and indifferent deity? Hardly. In a previous paragraph, he writes: "O LORD, be gracious to us; we long for you. Be our strength every morning, our salvation in time of distress" (v. 2).

*We long for you.*

Does your relationship with God fill you with longing?

Do you want a more personal relationship with God? The kind of relationship that can, indeed, serve as a foundation for your life? That can serve as a source of salvation, wisdom, and knowledge?

**Do fathers know best? Do mothers? No way. But there is one Father who does.**

There is one way to enter into intimate relationship with God: "For God so loved the world that he gave his one and only Son, that whoever believes in him shall not perish but have eternal life" . . . and "Jesus answered, 'I am the way and the truth and the life. No one comes to the Father except through me. If you really knew me, you would know my Father as well'" (John 3:16 and 14:6).

The key to knowing God is knowing Jesus Christ.

When we have a relationship with God's own Son, Jesus, we find ourselves adopted into the family of God. What we used to think of as some nebulous cosmic power suddenly becomes real to us in a way we never could have imagined. The Force becomes family. That higher power turns out to be a heavenly Father. We discover that the distant deity is more along the lines of . . . well, actually, a dad.

We've strayed a long way from the concept that you and I are clueless parents and, as such, could benefit from a little extra wisdom now and then.

But then again, maybe we haven't wandered far at all. The fact that we are as clueless and imperfect as we are—as parents and as human beings—well, it seems to underscore what the Bible has been telling us all along:

We need a heavenly Father in our lives to help us make sense of life . . . to help us meet the challenges of raising our families . . . to help us achieve our potential as parents, spouses, and human beings.

Best yet, it's not an empty hope. There really is a heavenly Father who loves us and who desires a more personal, intimate relationship with us.

Do fathers know best? Do mothers? No way. But there is one Father who does. Do you want to be the best possible parent to your children? Then become a child yourself. Become a child of God. Learn to call him "Dad." Get to know the Father who really does know best . . . your whole life will be enriched as a result.

 ## Moms and Dads . . . Wise Up!

Three steps to being a wiser parent:

**Reading.** Check out the Bible. There is an entire book devoted to the sayings of the wisest king who ever lived. Entitled *Proverbs,* it is truly a textbook for living wisely. Read it to yourself . . . to your spouse . . . to your children. The principles in these pages can help guide you through many of life's crossroads. Whether or not you consider yourself a "Christian," you will benefit from reading and applying the wisdom in these pages.

**Requesting.** There is a verse in the Book of James that talks about requesting wisdom. Paraphrased for parents, it might read: "If you are a clueless parent who lacks wisdom, ask God." How can we ask God for help? Through prayer. Pray about the decisions you're facing today. Mention them specifically. Also, pray for your skills as a parent. Ask God to give you wisdom as you face the challenges of raising your children and being a godly partner for your spouse.

**Relationship.** How well do you know the Person who gave King Solomon the wisdom you're reading about in the Book of Proverbs? How well do you know the Person you're approaching in prayer? Your *reading* and your *requests* will have the greatest impact when they take place in the context of a close, personal *relationship* with God.

# You Can't Get Pregnant While Breast-Feeding

 ecently I was on the phone with pregnant friend Lisa Hovingh at Baker Book House. I asked if she'd be at the next Christian Booksellers Convention.

"I'm still deciding," she said. "About that time, my baby will be six weeks old."

"Six weeks? Let's see. You might actually be sitting down without a pillow by then."

That, of course, started a conversation about the discomforts of childbirth. At one point Lisa, pregnant with her first baby, said, "I guess the delivery part's the pits."

"You've never been in such pain," I quipped. And then I laughed.

I can't believe I laughed.

Of course, it was the laugh of a mom who knows that the pain is eclipsed by the joy of holding your new infant, but I forgot to mention that part. I just laughed. I might as well have suggested she'd be in less pain if she spent the afternoon doing the splits—up to her neck. I just hope she wasn't too discouraged by our conversation. I'll feel bad if she talks her husband into a vasectomy before he's had a chance to change his first diaper.

But maybe it goes with the territory. During my first pregnancy I too was terrorized by delivery-room veterans. It seemed as though every mom had a story or comment related to my condition. Women told me about 52-hour labors and drug-free deliveries and levels of pain that made them grab their husbands by the collars and swear them to celibacy from that day forward. In truth, I spent a good part of my pregnancy longing for the days when I still believed all those stork-and-cabbage-leaf theories.

Whenever women discover that one of our own is "in the family way," we can't help ourselves. We rally together to inform, inspire, entertain and, yes, even terrify. Every mom has stories of the pain and magic of giving birth, not to mention all the stories—funny and poignant—floating around about pregnancy. And who doesn't have a half-dozen "old wives' tales" to share!

Picking through the sea of information can be challenging. Sometimes it helps to remember to approach it all with a grain of salt. After all, you can't always believe everything you hear. And when it's all said and done—when the maternity clothes are in a box in the attic and we've adequately populated our homes with offspring to nag and to love—what then? What have we learned from our season of maternity? Have our experiences prepared us somehow to be better mothers? Have they served a purpose other than providing us with children? Have they changed us, in some fashion, for the good?

## Prenatal Myths and Mysteries

When I was pregnant, well-meaning friends offered a mother lode of advice such as, "You can't get pregnant while breast-feeding," and "If you thread a needle and suspend it over your stomach, you can tell by the way it spins whether you're going to have a boy or a girl," and the all-time favorite, "Soda crackers reduce morning sickness."

Even the best women's magazines propagate that soda cracker story. Now, I'm certain that crackers work for many women. I'm just not one of them. I bought so many boxes of saltines the store manager began stocking a special aisle just for me. I ate crackers until I answered to the name "Polly." Nabisco still sends Christmas cards. And, nearly two years after my last pregnancy, I'm not even close to purging all the cracker crumbs from the corners of the bottoms of my purses.

And I still threw up.

Actually, I know women who have had it a lot worse than I did. One of my friends had morning sickness all day, every day, for four months. She threw up every single meal. The good news is that as soon as she threw up what she had just eaten, she felt better, creating a window of time for about an hour when she could eat something else and keep it down. When her husband wanted to take her to a pricey restaurant for her birthday, he made her eat at home before they left. He told her, "I'm not going to pay for an expensive meal so you can flush it down the toilet. As long as you're going to throw up, I'd rather it be cheap food from home." Sure enough, he waited until she threw up, then took her to a nice seafood restaurant.

Maybe it's not a mystery that pregnant women throw up. After all, when we're not throwing up, some of us are craving

*Another myth told to pregnant women is that we're eating for two. We forget that the person for whom we are scarfing down our second Big Mac weighs less than the box the hamburger came in.*

some pretty weird things. My sister Renee craved shaved ice. It was summer in Beeville, Texas, and she would waddle to a local snow cone stand and order a snow cone sans syrup. When she wasn't eating ice, she craved the smell of ice. Her husband, Harald, often found her in the kitchen, standing in front of the open freezer, smelling the vapors.

*I've been talking about myths and mysteries. The bad news is that the postnatal body is not a myth. The mystery is that some women who have experienced the postnatal body actually go on to have more children.*

My husband was truly shocked when, at two months into my pregnancy, I came home from Sam's Club with a five-gallon jug of pickles. He said, "I thought that pickle thing was just a myth."

Of course, that was my first pregnancy. I was young. I was naïve. Eight years later, pregnant with Kacie, I was far more savvy. I didn't crave pickles. I craved beef. Several times a month I'd announce, "Gee, I'm really craving beef" and Larry would take me out for a nice steak dinner. If I'm ever pregnant again, I think I'm going to crave a new sofa. Or flowers. Or maybe even cash.

Another myth often told to pregnant women is that we are eating for two. We forget that the person for whom we are scarfing down our second Big Mac weighs less than the box the hamburger came in. This is how a woman gets herself into the predicament of giving birth to a seven-pound baby and praying fervently that she'll deliver a forty-pound placenta to account for the rest of her prenatal poundage.

And what about that postnatal body?

I've been talking about myths and mysteries. The bad news is that the postnatal body is not a myth. The mystery is that some women who have experienced the postnatal body actually go on to have more children.

More than one woman has stood naked in front of the mirror after giving birth and wondered if what she's seeing could actually be THAT MANY stretch marks, or if her toddler has been scribbling with red lipstick on the mirror again. New moms sometimes fear that a hospital mix-up will send them home with the wrong baby. I knew I came home with the right baby—I was convinced, however, that I'd been sent home with the wrong body.

I remember, three or four days after bringing my second baby home from the hospital, becoming overwhelmed with the oddities of my postnatal body. It was two A.M. and I was sitting in a chair in my bedroom, trying to nurse a fussy baby with nipples that felt like they'd been through a meat tenderizer. When Larry woke up and asked me if everything was okay, he got more of an answer than he bargained for.

I blurted, "No, I'm not okay. My boobs hurt and my stitches hurt and my eyes sting from lack of sleep and I get these horrible contractions whenever I nurse and now I can't even go to the bathroom and I think I'm getting a bladder infection!" And I burst into tears.

## From Myths and Mysteries to Magic

And yet . . .

Despite morning sickness and weird cravings and stretch marks and pain, childbirth is cloaked in magic, isn't it? There is something almost otherworldly about the process of bringing a new baby into the world.

Remember the first time you saw your baby's face? Did you shed tears? I did. Did you forget about the pain and the blood and the indignities? Me, too.

Did you count fingers and toes? Trace the curve of a seashell ear? Marvel at the snug grip of translucent fingers wrapped around your thumb? Perhaps you stroked a downy cheek, soft as the wing of a bird, or let the tips of your fingers caress a tiny, rosebud mouth.

And you knew right then that your life would never be the same again. Oh, I'm not talking about the logistics of raising a child. I'm talking about the transformation of your very soul.

**Remember the first time you saw your baby's face? Did you shed tears? I did. Did you forget about the pain and the blood and the indignities? Me, too.**

It changed you, didn't it? I know it changed me. The experience of losing my figure to pregnancy, my religion during hard labor, and my heart as soon as I laid eyes on my babies, well, it touched a hidden core. It opened windows in my soul—not so much granting a new perspective of the world, but a new view within as I experienced feelings and perspectives that, until that moment, had yet to see the light of day.

Turns out I had a whole new world inside of me. Like Alice's Wonderland behind the looking glass, or Aslan's kingdom beyond the wardrobe door, the journey into motherhood took me to a place where familiar things weren't quite what they seemed. I thought that, as a wife, I knew what love and vulnerability and sacrifice looked like. But as a mother, these familiar emotions took on hues and intensities I had never dreamed possible.

### Pass the Kleenex

Did you used to cry at tender moments the way you do now that you're a mother? I was never much of a "crier" at movies. But now it seems as though my tear ducts have a life of their own. Suddenly movies, books, commercials, billboards, street signs, conversations with gas station attendants, and even supermarket fliers . . . all seem to have the power to reduce me to a state of sentimental slush.

Last week Kaitlyn read to me a page from a book called *Stone Fox,* in which ten-year-old Willy enters a dogsled race to save his grandfather's farm. Competing against grown men, Willy knows his most formidable opponent is a Native American named Stone Fox, an intimidating rival who has won every race as long as anyone can remember.

Mind you, I haven't read the book. I have no emotional investment in this story whatsoever. Kaitlyn merely caught me up on the plot before reading me the final page of the book in which Searchlight—Willy's lead dog and best friend—drops dead of a heart attack ten feet from the finish line. When Stone Fox, in second place, comes across the boy weeping over the body of his dog, he dismounts his sled, draws his rifle, and scrapes a line in the snow. As the remaining racers approach, Stone Fox warns, "If anybody crosses this line, I will shoot them."

He stands guard until Willy collects himself, picks up his dog, and carries him across the finish line to win the race.

As Kaitlyn finished reading, she was surprised by a honking sound coming from the end of the couch where I was sitting. She looked up in concern. "Mom?"

I was sobbing. SOBBING!

Would someone please tell me what is wrong with me? In fact, I'm teary-eyed now as I retell the story.

AND I HAVEN'T EVEN READ THE BOOK.

I don't think this is normal.

Yet other moms tell similar stories about becoming moved and teary at the oddest moments.

Why do we do this?

Maybe it's because, as adults, we know that life contains too few shining moments like the one depicted in this story. In our worlds of car pools and dishes and deadlines and bills, there is too little magic. And yet . . .

We know about the magic, don't we? If we are mothers, we know what it means to be touched by the very hand of heaven. In a delivery room six months ago or six years ago or sixty, we experienced a miracle of our own. And the sheer power of that miracle, even today, can leave us humbled and even teary whenever we glimpse the magic at work in the life of someone else.

## Teaching Our Kids the Value of Magic

Our children don't need us to teach them about the magic that life has to offer. With their vivid imaginations and youthful perspectives, most kids can teach us way more than we can teach them. I don't need to prompt Kaitlyn to see a fairy dwelling when she looks at a stone storage hut at a local park . . . or to become giddy with anticipation of Santa's arrival on Christmas Eve . . . or to lose herself in fanciful fabrications of exquisite plots and drama each time she emerges, frilled and dazzling, from the dress-up box in the den closet.

*If we are mothers, we know what it means to be touched by the very hand of heaven. And the sheer power of that miracle, even today, can leave us humbled and even teary.*

She knows how to do these things all by herself. She knows how to build snowmen that wink in the twilight, erect lemonade stands certain to draw crowds and make millions, and throw herself into a tickling match with an intensity that Custer, Washington, or Lee would have done well to emulate.

Kids understand magic.

At least for a while. Then they begin to grow up, and the magic seems silly all of a sudden. Sometimes they try to replace the innocent magic of youth with the fleeting rush of premature love and lust. Sometimes, as they mature, the disappointments of life eclipse, for a few years, the promise of magic, and they become disillusioned.

How can we help our kids hang on to that which they grasp so naturally in childhood?

We can't teach them about magic. They already know more than we do.

But we can help them understand the value of what they have. How? Here are some suggestions.

*Let your kids know you're never too old to believe in magic.* When grown-ups stay enchanted with life, it helps kids realize that it's okay to stay in touch with that part of themselves as they grow and mature. I felt sort of embarrassed when I dissolved into sobs after hearing three paragraphs of *Stone Fox.* But I guess my sentimentality wasn't such a bad thing for Kaitlyn to witness. It's okay to be moved and touched and amazed by life, and to let your kids know that you are.

*Create moments to share with your child.* A couple months ago my friend Linda Holland was staying at my home while in town on business. One night it

*Luckily for Kaitlyn, her dad was not so shortsighted. He donned snow gear and the two of them spent the next hour creating a Too Cool Snow Guy complete with a snazzy red hat and my favorite mirrored sunglasses.*

began to snow, which is how we found ourselves standing on my back porch at midnight, marveling at streamers of snowflakes spiraling against a charcoal sky. Linda said, "I've never seen snowflakes spiral like that!" and, indeed, there was something extraordinarily enchanting about the midnight scene.

"I've got to wake Kaitlyn!" I said, hurrying into the house and up the stairwell. At her bedside, I nudged her and whispered her name. We sat together in the wicker loveseat beneath her bedroom window, gazing at the winter wonderland unfolding before our eyes. Wrapped in my arms, Kaitlyn felt warm from her bedclothes as she rubbed her sleepy eyes and spoke in whispers so as not to wake Kacie sleeping in the crib in the corner.

It didn't take long for Kaitlyn's eyes to grow heavy, and she tottered back to bed. The moment lasted less than five minutes. But the memory will last a lifetime.

Look for enchanting moments that appeal to you; then invite your children to share in your discoveries.

*Let your child create moments for you.* It's one thing to take time to smell the roses and enjoy the magic of life when I'm the one setting the agenda. But can I be flexible and learn to respond when my kids are the ones taking the initiative? Several weeks after I invited Kaitlyn to share my enchanting discovery, Duncanville experienced another snowfall and Kaitlyn invited me to venture into her world and build a snowman. I'm ashamed to say that I was too comfortable in my warm den, watching *Home Improvement.* I turned her down.

**Life is hard. It's filled with challenges and problems galore. But it's also filled with adventure and romance, mystery and magic, heart and soul.**

Luckily for Kaitlyn, her dad was not so shortsighted. He donned snow gear and the two of them spent the next hour creating a Too Cool Snow Guy complete with a snazzy red hat and my favorite mirrored sunglasses (I guess I deserved it).

Life is hard. It's filled with challenges and problems galore. But it's also filled with adventure and romance, mystery and magic, heart and soul. Bringing a baby into this world provides one of the best examples I can think of when the ordinary is eclipsed by the extraordinary, when the mundane makes room for the marvelous, when the practical nature of life dims beside the poetry of our existence.

If our season of maternity teaches us anything at all, it's that sometimes heaven touches earth. Miracles still happen.

It's okay to be sentimental. Even grown-ups can be enchanted with life. And we're never too old to believe in magic.

And that, my friend, is worth the price of a stretch mark any day.

## Savoring Life's Magic Moments

Life is filled with mystery and magic. One of the greatest privileges of family life is getting to experience all that mystery and magic with people we love the most. Unfortunately, acknowledging the whimsical, sentimental aspects of life doesn't always come naturally, expecially as we cross the bridge of years and find that we have exchanged our decoder rings, Pooh Bear tea sets, and Nancy Drew mysteries for bathtub rings, Noritake, and *Consumer Reports*.

I'd like you to do three things. *First, make a list of Kodak moments from your childhood*—experiences or events that held some magic for you. Remembering enchanting moments from your past just may be the key to becoming more aware of magical moments in the present!

My list would include the times my parents woke my sisters and me up in the middle of the night for midnight excursions to Bob's Big Boy for hot chocolate . . . or the smell of my dad's cologne and my mom's perfume on the nights they were going out to dinner (and the way the fragrance lingered on my clothes after I hugged them good-bye) . . . or the night I got my first kiss from a boy: I was thirteen, he worked at Taco Bell and had just dedicated the song "The Most Beautiful Girl in the World" to me on our local radio station . . .

*Now think about your years as an adult.* Are there any experiences that evoke similar feelings today? For me, there's something special about fresh cut flowers on my kitchen table. Reading classic books to my daughters can feel enchanting as well (*Peter Pan* is a favorite). Watching the moon slowdance across the sky from my back-porch swing always makes me feel connected with the magic and mystery of the world in which we live.

*Finally, this week, do one thing that evokes these kinds of feelings for you.*

God created a world that is, indeed, enchanting and wonderful. In fact, the Bible says that you and I are fearfully and wonderfully made. If we know what to look for, we just might discover that we didn't grow up and leave it all behind after all. Oh sure, it's unavoidable that life will, at times, feel maddening or mundane. And yet, plenty of mystery, magic, and miracles remain as well.

# Myth #9

# There's No Place like Home

'll tell you what's wrong with America today: Our symbol of the good life needs to be revised.

All across the United States, families are focusing their energies on the American Dream of owning their own home. Once we achieve that goal, we keep working toward variations of the same theme: a bigger house, landscaped yard, motor home in the driveway, gated entrance, backyard pool, and eventually even maid's quarters occupied by an actual maid.

While we are pursuing this dream, other countries are focusing on vastly different priorities. The goal in Japan is to get a good education. Citizens in China dream about traveling abroad. The French want to be good lovers. The British expend their energy following the antics of the royal family.

Notice that several of these other goals are productive. And if they aren't productive, at least they don't consume a lot of energy or time. For example, three to five belly-laughs at the expense of the Prince of Wales consume less than twenty-five calories. And making love, despite what Hollywood portrays, is not an all-day affair. (In fact, the longer you've been married, the less time it takes. One friend confided that she and her husband used to make love for hours. Then an hour. Then twenty minutes. Now they wrap things up before the commercial ends and David Letterman comes back on the air. She's looking forward to the time when sex takes place so quickly it creates a time warp and consumes "negative time," adding much-needed minutes back into her day.)

Maybe this is why other countries are starting to pull ahead of us in technology, scientific advancements, and industry. Citizens from other nations have more time and energy than we do. This is because the American Dream is both unproductive and time-consuming. The average home in America costs one hundred thousand dollars, so you can see that it takes vast quantities of resources and time to buy a home in the first place. And that's the easy part: It takes even more resources and time to maintain it once it's yours.

## Don't Try This at Home

There's something enriching about owning your own home, and the people getting richest are owners of your local hardware store. They make a pretty decent living telling people like you and me that we can do it ourselves, when what they really mean is that we can do it ourselves if we have no pride of ownership and don't mind that the redwood deck that took a month of Sundays to build would win honorable mention at a modern arts festival.

For some reason, home ownership is synonymous with trying to accomplish feats best left to the professionals. In my opinion, repairing a broken pipe, hanging crown molding, or insulating an attic are on par with performing plastic surgery and should not be attempted by average homeowners, no matter how much free time they have on their hands.

I know that do-it-yourself home improvements are alluring. There's something hypnotic about watching Bob Vila caulk bathtubs on The Learning Channel, not to mention the fact that Tim Allen wields hammers and humor in a manner that few can resist. But we just have to be strong. We can learn how to say no. Homer the Home Depot cartoon mascot may make projects seem easy in his weekly flier, but that's his job. That's why he gets paid the big bucks. You, on the other hand, don't get paid diddly. And if you're a stay-at-home mom, you don't get paid at all. So my best advice to you is to try to abstain.

*Sure we can do-it-ourselves if we have no pride of ownership and don't mind that the redwood deck that took a month of Sundays to build would win honorable mention at a modern arts festival.*

I'm sorry. I don't mean to be unreasonable. No doubt there will be moments when the lure of a do-it-yourself project will be too great and you will succumb. When this happens, there are a few things you need to remember:

1. The word *emergency* is relative. The people at 911 will not consider a broken pipe to be an emergency at any time of the day or night. Your local plumber, however, considers any plumbing problem that occurs after five o'clock to be an emergency, and will bill you accordingly. In other words, if it is Thursday night, and you are installing a garbage disposal when a pipe breaks and floods your home, your first call should be to the

plumber. Your next call should be to 911. Be prepared to do this as soon as the plumber hands you his bill. This is permissible because coronaries are considered emergencies by every profession.

2. Sometimes projects done incorrectly can still be salvaged. The trick is to look on the bright side. Ceramic tile laid upside down, for example, has a rougher texture and will provide better traction when wet.

3. The best way to find a dropped nail or any other dangerous object lost in the pile of your carpet is to let a two-year-old loose in the room. She will immediately run pell-mell toward the dangerous object in question. Your job is to grab it before she does.

4. Do not let your ten-year-old give herself a manicure with a product labeled "Liquid Nails" no matter how much she begs.

5. The installation time printed on the box containing your new garbage disposal is not related to the amount of time it will take to actually install the product. In fact, installation estimates are derived by multiplying the number of bathrooms at the company warehouse by the age of the oldest secretary on the premises, and dividing that figure by the amount of the last settlement paid to a disgruntled employee. If you want an accurate picture of the time it will take to install something, you need to use a different formula altogether: Calculate the worst-case-scenario amount of time you would be willing to spend on this project, then multiply by four.

6. Do not peer into a staple gun and pull the trigger to see if there are any staples in it.

7. You cannot take a wad of Plumber's Putty, press it onto a newspaper comic strip, and transfer the image to another piece of paper. Likewise, you cannot use Silly Putty to seal the pipes under the kitchen sink.

8. You can incorporate workshop tools into your personal care and hygiene regimen if you follow a few safety guidelines: First, when using an electric sander to massage sore muscles, it helps to remove the sandpaper. Also, when using the same tool instead of buffing creme to slough off those annoying dead skin cells, leave the sandpaper in place, but do not—I repeat, DO NOT—use an extension cord to take the sander with you into the shower. This will short-out your sander and leave a very nasty burnt smell in your bathroom, not to mention sloughing off skin cells that weren't even close to being dead yet.

*Sometimes projects done incorrectly can still be salvaged. The trick is to look on the bright side. Ceramic tile laid upside down, for example, has a rougher texture and will provide better traction when wet.*

9. Remember when as kids we used to pour rubber cement on our hands, let it dry, then roll it into little rubber balls? Don't try this with the glue from a glue gun.

10. When building bookshelves, fixing things, or doing other odd jobs around the house, follow the universal guideline espoused by successful contractors, tailors, and even plastic surgeons: "Measure twice, cut once."

## When You Need to Call a Professional

If you don't want the stress and frustration of "doing it yourself," an alternative is to hire a professional. Lots of people hire professionals and are happy with the experience. In fact, they all get together at a national convention each year to share stories. I think this year they're convening at Wendy's.

Unfortunately, not every encounter between homeowner and professional has such a happy ending. A number of years ago I flew home to visit my folks and spotted my dad toting a gun beneath his sports coat. Turns out he was being stalked by a roofing contractor who was furious at not getting paid for a botched job. The roofer had used the wrong kind of nails, turning an open-beamed ceiling into an inverted bed of nails and causing the roof to leak like a sieve.

But I don't want to discourage you from taking this approach. The chances are very good that you will not be stalked by your contractor. In fact, you might even get a good laugh out of the experience. Our friends Larry and Nancy did.

Larry and Nancy Rottmeyer relocated to our area recently when Larry was named Dean of the School of Business at Dallas Baptist University. They purchased a home and immediately began planning their redecorating strategy. They figured with a little ceramic tile, paint, and wallpaper, they would be the proud owners of a dream-house come true.

Luckily, Larry and Nancy understand the insidious threat of do-it-yourself projects. Did they consider painting the inside of their home themselves? Let's just say that Howard Stern spends more time reading Emily Post than Larry and Nancy spent thinking about "doing it themselves."

They took the high road and hired professionals.

They probably made the right decision. I also think there are moments in life when the right decision goes so terribly wrong you begin to hope the worst thing that happens is that you spend several years in therapy.

What was supposed to be a five-day job ended up stretching over four weeks. The painters began by instructing my friends to empty the contents of their bedroom closets into the living room. Larry and Nancy assumed this meant the closets were to be painted first. They were wrong. Within hours of arriving, the painters had spray painted the living room. But, hey, it was a neutral color so the speckles didn't show up too bad on the clothes.

Out of the promised crew of six, some days one person showed up, some days none. But perhaps the most telling discovery was learning the reason behind one crew member's excessive protective gear and breathing masks: she's allergic to paint.

When it was all over, Nancy only had to repaint one bathroom, and Larry took to the keyboard looking for a way to glean a smile from the comedy of errors. After he published a description of the experience in a family newsletter, my guess is that Home Depot experienced a notable increase in paint sales to converted do-it-yourselfers. I asked permission to excerpt part of that newsletter for this chapter, and here it is:

According to Larry Rottmeyer, you know the painters have been at your home too long when . . .

- . . . you begin to receive their mail forwarded to your home.
- . . . you are charged a late fee at Blockbuster for their last video.
- . . . they begin to eat the middle out of your Oreos.
- . . . you draw their names in your family Christmas gift draw.
- . . . the IRS informs you that you can claim them as dependents.
- . . . your mom calls and asks to talk with them.
- . . . if they're not there, Mom says she'll call back.

## The Grass Is Always Greener after a Really Good Rain

As if household repairs aren't daunting enough, if you own your own home, there's a good chance that it came with a yard. This means yard work. Our house, for example, came with nearly an acre. I can look out my windows and pretend I'm living in a park. Unfortunately, city gardeners didn't come with the deal.

When we bought this home, we had just moved from a postage-stamp-sized lot in Southern California. The day escrow closed, I looked at the wide open spaces between the back door and backyard fence and told Larry, "We need to buy a riding mower."

He scoffed. "With what? We sank every dollar into the down payment."

"They're about a thousand dollars. Let's put it on the credit card."

"No way. You know how I feel about running a balance on the credit card. If we buy a mower, we'll do it with cash."

"We don't have the cash."

"Then we'll save until we do."

The next Saturday morning, Larry donned his work-clothes and went into the backyard. His goal was to tame the Texas prairie taking shape behind our house. His tool of choice: the little push mower we'd brought with us from California.

I heard the mower spring to life around nine thirty. At eleven I sent Kaitlyn out with a Dr Pepper and the suggestion to take a break. She returned empty-handed, the mower puttering on.

At noon I waved Larry inside for his favorite lunch of Campbell's bean with bacon soup and Ritz crackers. He ate without comment, a determined look on his face. Ten minutes later the mower coughed back into action.

I served dinner at sunset. It was silent outside when I went to find Larry. He was clearing brush near the back fence so he could—you guessed it—keep mowing. He sent me back into the house, alone.

The tired little mower droned on until nearly eight, just as a spring thunderstorm blew in from the east and small droplets began to hit the roof. When my husband walked into the kitchen a few minutes later, I thought one of the backyard shrubs had pulled up roots and come in from the rain. I peered beneath the facade of dirt and grass several moments before glimpsing the man I had married.

The next day was Sunday. It would have been nice to have spent the afternoon picnicking on our parklike lawn, but we weren't even home. We were across town, shopping. Actually, we were at Home Depot. With our VISA.

Buying a riding mower.

## Tools Can Make the House . . .

Houses require a lot of work. Between plumbing and painting and gardening and decorating, sometimes it feels as though we hardly have any time to enjoy our humble abodes.

Don't get me wrong. There's actually a lot to be said for hard work. It can be therapeutic. It teaches discipline. The thrill of accomplishment builds confidence. Work can even be an act of worship to the God who gives us energy, health, projects and possessions, goals and dreams. Work can actually be viewed as a privilege—not to mention the fact that there's something to be said for responsible stewardship of the possessions entrusted to our care.

Still . . .

If we're not careful . . .

It's possible for us to maintain, upgrade, fix, and repair to within an inch of our lives and still not hit the nail on the head. We can measure on Monday, trowel on Tuesday, weed on Wednesday, trim on Thursday, fertilize on Friday, solder on Saturday, sand on Sunday . . . and still have little to show for our efforts but a nice house. It will be a fancy shell, to be sure, but nothing more than that. Just a house.

Toolbox in hand, we can make a house a house.

But how do we make a house a home?

117

## . . . But It Takes Love to Make a Home

My guess is that every family has a different list of what it takes to make a house a home. And yet, I'd wager that our lists would have many elements in common. What does it take to make a home? How about . . .

### *Familiar Things*

I read an article once about a family that moved frequently due to sad circumstances. Just as everyone began to feel settled, dad's drinking and debts would prompt yet another relocation. The author of the article—once a child in this home—told about his mother's one odd passion: after every move, there was one box she unpacked before any other. Before reclaiming bed sheets or flatware or clothes, she made a beeline for the box marked "curtains." Within minutes, she identified which curtains from her stockpile would fit which windows and proceeded to hang the well-worn fabric. He and his brothers laughed at their mother's obsession . . . until the day he figured out what she was doing. He realized that his mother was giving her family the best gift she could: the gift of familiarity in strange surroundings. In Arkansas or Phoenix, Dallas or New Orleans, each new dwelling bore a striking resemblance to the last in one single manner. For this family—and particularly for one young boy—curtains made it home.

*Is your home the backdrop for celebration? Food, friends, and fellowship can turn any dwelling into a home.*

Is there a way for you and me to highlight familiar things in our homes? Here are some ideas:

- I heard of one woman who recycled all of her toddler's favorite playclothes once they became too worn or

118

stained for use. She cut squares from the familiar fabric and pieced together an inviting quilt for her child to enjoy.

- Displaying family photos can help make a house a home. I tend to shun portraits and opt instead to enlarge favorite snapshots that reveal more in their candid nature than any pose could ever do! I also splurge on quality, classic-looking frames in a variety of styles and sizes, then group the photos on a desk, end table, or mantel.

- Kids' artwork can add a whimsical and familiar touch. One friend is proud of her refrigerator art gallery. I select favorite creations and have them framed. It's expensive, but worth the investment. I also tack artwork inside the doors of my kitchen cabinets for an unexpected warm-fuzzy while reaching for a can of Spaghettios.

- Can Grandma's quilt work as a wall hanging in the dining room? Can you display your dad's coin collection on the bookshelf in the den? Where might your great-aunt's doilies add a homey touch? Heirlooms and collections from family members are another way to personalize your home with familiar things.

## Celebrations

Is your home the backdrop for celebration? Food, friends, and fellowship can turn any dwelling into a home. Sometimes our celebrations are the standard fare, such as birthdays and holidays. But don't bypass the opportunity to recognize other important events: the removal of braces, a promotion at work, report card improvements, completion of a tough school assignment, and more.

The dinner hour can be a great time to host an impromptu celebration. To help you create a party atmosphere on short notice, keep a celebration box stocked with goodies such as:

- *Candies and confetti.* One woman creates a party atmosphere by sprinkling her dinner table with confetti laced with something sweet: M&M's, Skittles, Hershey's Kisses, or Gummi Bears. As soon as her family convenes at the kitchen table for dinner, they know something special is being recognized. It's also the one circumstance in which she lets her kids snack before dinner: When there's something to celebrate and her kids eyeball the candy and ask, "Mom, can we . . . ?" this mom smiles and says yes.

- *Crepe paper streamers and a roll of masking tape.* It doesn't take much time to twist some streamers across a room.

- *Paint pens.* National chain MJ Designs sells, in their art department, a paint pen for writing on glass and windows. Even as I speak, the glass panels in my kitchen French doors are decorated with Kaitlyn's artwork in this fashion—what a quick, festive way to emblazon a celebratory message! In fact, I bought the pen to ink birthday greetings on the car windshield of "aging" friend Mike Talley. Best yet, the paint wipes off with a wet cloth. Decorate windows in your kitchen, at the office, on a car . . . even bathroom mirrors are fair game!

- *Cardboard balloons.* Balloons add so much color and life, but they are time-consuming to inflate. As an alternative, I purchased colored file folders in hues of purple, green, and yellow, then cut each folder into two ovals to create reusable cardboard balloons. I even tied curling ribbon to the bottom of each balloon. I tape them around the walls in my kitchen for a party atmosphere that doesn't leave me rubbing tired cheeks.

- *A bottle of sparkling apple cider.* Carbonated apple juice adds a festive touch, especially when served in fancy glassware.

120

- *"You Are Special" mug or plate.* You may have seen the red "You Are Special" dinnerware. We have a mug, but I've seen plates as well. You don't need both . . . either mug or dish adorning the place setting of a family member who has just accomplished something special will say a lot.
- *Greeting cards.* Keep a stock of congratulatory cards. I have some that say: "You Are Special," "Congratulations! You Did It!" and "Way to Go!" Have family members sign a card and put it on the dinner plate of the person you want to honor.
- *Paper crown.* What better way to make someone feel like a queen or king for the day!

## Family Traditions

Familiar rituals provide an instant point of connection. They have the power to transport family members from their separate, harried worlds to a shared place where good memories mingle with the promise of good things to come.

Shirley Mitchell, for example, recalls that when she was raising her four children, she sometimes noticed that they were spending too much time with friends and that family unity was suffering. Whenever this happened, Shirley planned a camp-out. For a weekend or week, the family slept in a tent, blazed trails, played games, shared dreams around the campfire, and came home refreshed and realigned with one another.

The Rottmeyers celebrate every Friday with their adolescent children by going out to dinner and coming home to videos and popcorn. Mike and Darla Talley make a holiday tradition of driving to a tree farm and cutting a fresh Christmas tree each December. Dave Watson cooks French toast for his wife and children every Saturday morning without fail.

No matter where you are—in your home, on vacation, or in the middle of relocating to a new city and state—enjoying a familiar ritual with your family can make you feel at home.

And sometimes, a familiar ritual can do even more than that. When I was growing up, a favorite ritual was for my two sisters and me to engage my dad in a wrestling match/tickle fest. He would protest and say he was too tired, but once he took off his glasses and set them carefully out of the way, we knew the fun was about to begin. Years later, I was sitting on the couch one evening with my own family when my six-year-old daughter challenged her dad to a wrestling match. When Larry took off his glasses and set them carefully out of the way, I experienced a rush of emotion that, even today, is hard to put into words. And for just a heartbeat I was home again, six-years-old-and-counting, cocky and secure in the bear hug of a hero-dad.

Do you want to experience the joy of owning a house? There is pride and satisfaction that comes with home ownership—but it's not uncommon for the good feelings to be tempered at times by frustration and expense!

To experience joy of a more permanent nature, make a *home*. Whether you live in a duplex, apartment, trailer park, or house . . . raised cottage or saltbox or Victorian gem, focus your efforts on creating an atmosphere that invites people in and nurtures them once they're there.

That, after all, is what a home is all about.

# Myth #10

## Silence Is Golden

They say that silence is golden, but I'm not too sure. Maybe there are stages of family life when this is true, like retirement.

But for families with children, silence can be anything but golden.

The last time I experienced a few moments of silence in my home, I walked into the kitchen to discover that Kacie had managed to set the microwave on fire. Of course, she was able to fit this activity into her busy schedule because she had some downtime after her morning excursion, which was to give the cordless phone a bath in the toilet.

My friend Jackie O'Brian is blessed with a child who makes the Roadrunner look like a geriatric patient with iron-poor blood. When Casey was not yet two, he was supposed to be in the backyard raking leaves with his dad when the silence became noticeably alarming. His folks searched for him in the backyard, front yard, house, garden . . . to no avail. They were about ready to launch a door-to-door search when they heard a shout and turned to see Casey being lugged homeward in the arms of a seventeen-year-old neighbor kid who lived across the street and several houses away. This young man was heading to work when he approached his red pickup sitting in the driveway of his home, opened the door, and discovered Casey sitting behind the wheel.

Casey's fascination with cars remains a challenge. One day he watched his dad mix grout to tile a bathroom floor. The next day, two-year-old Casey let himself into the garage, mixed up a fresh batch of grout, and grouted the front end of the family van.

Are these stories unusual? Hardly. In fact, anyone who has been a parent more than five minutes knows that even a heartbeat of silence in a household peopled with small children can be a spine-chilling experience.

## Safety First

As a parent of a toddler, my first responsibility is to keep my child safe from bodily harm. My second responsibility is to keep her from leveling our home. To help me meet these goals, there exists a vast spectrum of child-safety devices on the market today.

Most of the time these devices help me meet both goals at the same time: They protect my baby *and* they protect my house. Sometimes, however, you have to choose between your baby and your possessions.

Last year I came home after spending a week in California and discovered that Larry had childproofed the entire house. Then again, the word *childproof* may be a misnomer. I suspect that even escape artist David Copperfield couldn't move freely around our home.

Larry had managed to scrounge up protective devices that I never even knew existed. When he gave me a tour of our newly secured home, I was impressed—at first. As we walked from room to room, Larry demonstrated the new devices, and I responded to his ingenuity.

In the kitchen, I praised the plastic locks on the cabinets.

In the den, I expressed appreciation for the new Velcro thingamajig that restricts access to our entertainment center.

In the bathroom, I forced a thin smile at the fact that I can no longer raise the toilet lid unless I return to college and obtain a degree in mechanical engineering.

About this time, I realized the experience was going downhill fast. It crashed and burned, however, in the living room where I discovered that Larry had mounted plastic protectors on the corners of my prized, four-hundred-dollar, hand-painted and customized coffee table—and that he had committed this heinous act of hostility against a helpless home furnishing using SCREWS.

*As a parent of a toddler, my first responsibility is to keep my child safe from bodily harm. My second responsibility is to keep her from leveling our home.*

I coughed. "Did the instructions tell you to actually SCREW the plastic into the sides of the table?" I was hoping he'd say yes. Between replacement cost and emotional trauma I figured I could pull in at least a couple thousand.

Larry beamed. "No way! They included some adhesive stuff guaranteed not to permanently mar your furniture. But the tape didn't stick well, and I spent an hour trying to mount those things until it dawned on me to use screws!"

He stopped. I think he was waiting for applause.

But I was too preoccupied to clap. Actually, I was thinking that with a *true* jury of my peers (meaning other women who know the value of a coffee table) I'd be acquitted for sure.

## It's All in Your Head

As our kids grow, physical safety becomes less of an issue. Oh, we still make them wear seatbelts and bike helmets and look both ways before they cross the street. But at some point, guarding their bodies seems to require far less vigilance than guarding other, less tangible things.

Like what? How about their minds? Or their attitudes? And if that's not nebulous enough for you, how about their moral development, belief systems, and even their very souls?

Here's where companies are missing the boat. We don't need a new-and-improved child gate. We need a mind sensor that tells us when our kids are formulating an elaborate lie to explain why Muffy the poodle has suddenly gone a shade of brunette that looks suspiciously like the model on the box of Clairol we bought last week and stashed in the bathroom cabinet.

*Believe it or not, I couldn't locate a single company offering curfew enhancement cuffs that deliver intermittent low-grade electrical shocks if a kid isn't home before eleven, or even a peer-neutralizing aerosol spray guaranteed, with one spritz, to eliminate bad-influence friends.*

We don't need glow-in-the-dark toilet seat locks. We need a facial harness that locks up tight at the first hint of a rude, sarcastic comment emerging from the lips of our adolescent darlings.

The world will survive without another version of a VCR protector that keeps toddlers from jamming building blocks into the tape receptacle. We are in dire need, however, of a protection device that hinders our teens from filling their minds with media images of illicit sex, violence, and self-gratification.

Unfortunately, Corporate America isn't rising to the challenge. There's a real vacuum on the market today of innovative products guaranteed to help us protect the hearts and souls and minds of the children we love. Believe it or not, I couldn't locate a single company offering curfew enhancement cuffs that deliver intermittent low-grade electrical shocks if a kid isn't home before eleven . . . or full-body chastity casts for hormonally driven teens . . . or even a peer-neutralizing aerosol spray guaranteed, with one spritz, to eliminate bad-influence friends.

## Ideas That Work

It's too bad we can't exchange the names of companies marketing REALLY useful products to parents of adolescents and teens. But if we can't exchange catalogs, maybe we can exchange ideas. How can we guard our kids once they're too big to benefit from outlet covers and cabinet latches?

### *On Curfews*

If you're tired of waiting up to see if your kids make curfew, put an alarm clock outside your bedroom door, poised to ring at the curfew hour. Your son or daughter will be able to turn off the alarm before it sounds—if he or she is home in time!

My parents used a different approach. The rule was that my sisters and I had to knock on the bedroom door and wake my parents when we came home at night—no matter what time it was. My mom kept, on her nightstand, a digital clock with a four-inch glow-in-the-dark display that was capable of burning numeric images into the sleepiest of brains. Next morning we'd have a conversation like this: She'd say, "When did you get in last night?" I'd say, "Oh, I don't know. I think it was about 11:30." She'd say, "Try 12:09."

Busted.

### On Accountability

Karen Franklin says that she makes her teens fill her in on the "whys" (who, what, where, when) each time they leave home, as well as call her during the evening if there is any change of plans. When her teens complain, she reminds them that this kind of communication is a common courtesy practiced even between parents. Another veteran mom suggests getting Caller ID, a monitoring system that displays the phone number and name of each incoming call. The idea actually came from her prodigal daughter who admitted, "There were so many times I'd 'check in' and say I was at so-and-so's house when I was really at a phone booth. I really wish we'd had Caller ID to help keep me honest!"

*When a dating relationship went bust, my boyfriends were often more despondent over losing contact with my parents than they were over losing me.*

And while accountability thrives on communication between parent and child, it can also be enhanced with communication between parents. Karen says she stays in touch with parents of her children's friends. And when her children come home with a new friend, Karen often rings up the parents for a casual introduction.

### On Building Relationships

When your kids are young, begin the practice of building relationships with their friends.

- Encourage your child to invite friends to your home.
- During each visit, spend five or ten minutes visiting with your children and their friends about their world

(make sure you come across "interested" and not "interrogative").

- Invite friends to join your family for fun events, such as a day at Six Flags or an evening at the movies (make sure you pick up all expenses).
- Volunteer to provide car pool services, supervision, or snacks for school field trips or parties.
- Make a point to meet the parents of friends.
- Keep your home open and inviting, and well-stocked with videos, games, and snack-food favorites to encourage older kids to spend time there rather than somewhere less supervised.

When I was growing up, my parents followed these guidelines. Throughout junior high, high school, and even college, they provided all the Cokes and party food my friends and I could consume; as a result, it was much more fun (and less expensive) for my friends to spend time at my house than anywhere else.

My parents also made a point to connect one-on-one with many of my friends, asking questions about hobbies or interests, joking around, even telling stories on me! More than a few friends ended up calling my folks "Mom" and "Dad," and when a dating relationship went bust, boyfriends were often more despondent over losing contact with my parents than they were over losing me.

While spending time with your child and her friends is important, so is privacy. Kids need space to do their own thing without old fogies like us hanging over their shoulders. After greeting my party guests, my folks often retreated to their study. At one point, my parents even converted our garage to a game room so my friends and I had our own "space"— cameo appearances by parents, however, were both frequent and welcome.

What's the point of all this effort? What do you and your child get out of it? For one thing, having a working knowledge of your children's friends gives you a better chance of spotting potential peer-related problems before they start. Also, friends who dislike authority (and might influence your child to do likewise) will often weed themselves out of this kind of environment. Finally, your interest and presence reminds your child that she is, first and foremost, a member of your household, and that friendships need to take place within the context of the greater priority of family.

## On Prayer

How can we keep our kids safe?

We can guard their minds and screen their friends and shield their values and even shape their souls. And yet the bottom line, for every parent, is that we still fall far short of being able to adequately protect our kids from all that life brings their way.

Let prayer stand in the gap.

In my book *The Parent Warrior: Doing Spiritual Battle for Your Children* I observe:

> I am convinced that God is calling parents to take up spiritual arms for their children. Indeed, I believe that today's mothers and fathers *must* become impassioned interceders if we are to have any shot at all of raising children who are spiritually, emotionally, physically and socially whole.

I know a couple who are in the process of raising four children between the ages of eight and twenty. Their second child, now nineteen, is a godly young woman with a heart for spiritual things. But this wasn't always the case. For four years she lived, in the words of her mother, "in a far country" of anger, sex, and rebellion. During this time, Jean recalls that prayer was the only guardian influence she had over her wandering daughter.

"Sometimes God would bring a picture to my mind of a lost sheep in various dangerous situations, and this helped me know how to pray. Sometimes the little sheep would be cold and lonely, and I would pray that God would remind Lauralee that she could always turn to him for warmth and comfort. Sometimes the little sheep would be standing at the edge of a cliff, and I would pray for God to go get her, pulling her away from whatever imminent danger she was facing. At other times the little sheep was being lured into danger, and I asked him to speak truth in her ears and block the word of the Enemy from speaking deception into her heart.

"For four years, I stood on God's Word where he says that his sheep hear his voice. I knew Lauralee accepted Jesus into her life at an early age. I prayed, 'Lord, you said your sheep hear your voice, and she is one of your sheep. Speak to her. Bring her back like the lost sheep in the parable.'"

God answered that prayer.

The good news is that prayer warriors aren't born, they are made. We can ask God's Holy Spirit to teach us how to be prayer warriors for our children, bringing their names and their lives daily before our loving and protective God.

## Let God's Word Show You How to Pray for Your Children

Do you want your prayers for your children to be effective? The Bible gives us a wonderful promise in 1 John 5:14–15. God's Word promises that if we pray for things that are God's will for us, God will not only hear our prayer, but he will also give us what we are praying for!

How can we know what God's will is for our children? Well, the Bible is a wellspring of information when it comes to God's will for our lives and for the lives of our kids. In fact, to make doubly sure that we are praying according to God's will, why not take his own words, paraphrase them, and incorporate them into our prayers.

Here's an example: In Hebrews 13:20–21 Paul records one of his prayers for his spiritual children. "May the God of peace, who . . . brought back from the dead our Lord Jesus . . . equip you with everything good for doing his will, and may he work in us what is pleasing to him, through Jesus Christ, to whom be glory for ever and ever. Amen."

What a powerful prayer to adapt—virtually verbatim—for my own children!

*Dear heavenly Father, I know that you are the God of peace who is so powerful, you even brought Jesus back from the dead. I ask that you equip Kaitlyn with everything she needs to do your will. I ask that you would fashion her and work in her so that her life is pleasing to you, and that you would do these things through Jesus Christ, to whom be glory for ever and ever. Amen.*

I might even add, according to Romans 12:2: *Father, I ask that Kaitlyn would not be conformed to this world, but that she would be transformed by the renewing of her mind, that she might prove what is your good and acceptable and perfect will in her life.*

And on another day I might choose to pray from 2 Timothy 2:22: *Father, please give Kaitlyn the strength to flee youthful lusts. Give her the desire to pursue righteousness, faith, love, and peace.*

# You're Not Getting Older, You're Getting Better

Whoever coined this phrase must have Geritol tablets for brain cells. Of course we're getting older. By the minute.

How do I know that I'm losing the battle of the years? Well, let me ask you something: Would a younger, more vibrant woman try to open her car trunk using a set of plastic teething keys belonging to her baby?

Would the bathroom of a more youthful woman resemble the cosmetic counter of a major department store?

Would someone in the springtime of her youth nod off during the climax of a movie entitled *Cliffhanger*?

Of course not.

133

No, I don't think I'm being paranoid at all when I look furtively over my shoulder and say that Father Time and Mother Nature have joined forces and are out to get me. I've tried seeking refuge with Oil of Olay, asylum with Clairol, but to no avail. If I thought the Witness Protection Program could help me, I'd be writing this book under a pseudonym.

But time and nature keep catching up with me.

I guess no one's immune. You and I both know there's no fountain of youth. We know that time stands still for no one, that we're all rushing pell-mell through the seasons of our lives. And yet we're still surprised, aren't we? We are completely unprepared for that first wrinkle or initial gray hair or the first time the optometrist has the unmitigated nerve to suggest bifocals.

> *Our heart stops the first time we watch a five-year-old board a yellow school bus . . . or see a daughter in high heels . . . or hear a son's unbridled ecstasy the first time he answers the phone and is mistaken for his dad.*

You know what else we are completely unprepared for?

Time and nature as they relate to our children.

You know it's true. Theoretically, we understand and accept the idea that our children are going to grow up. And yet our heart stops the first time we watch a five-year-old board a yellow school bus . . . or see a daughter in high heels . . . or hear a son's unbridled ecstasy the first time he answers the phone and is mistaken for his dad.

Several weeks ago Kaitlyn turned ten. In honor of the occasion, we planned a surprise midnight tea party for Kaitlyn and three overnight guests. The four girls were asleep by 10:30 (unaware that their slumber would be short-lived). I then spent the next hour transforming my dining room into a candlelit tea room. I pulled out all the stops: my best china, linens, cookies, and candies . . . and at each place setting a velvet box containing a silver heart necklace. It was supposed to be fun. I had no idea that, while folding a napkin, I would be seized with emotion, blurt "My baby's turning ten!" and begin to cry.

We look forward to the milestones, and yet they take us by surprise all the same.

## Making Memories

The thing I don't want is to look back from the vantage point of an empty nest and realize that I didn't appreciate what I had while I had it. Time is marching on—for you and for me, and for our families as well. We can't keep our kids from growing up and out from under our wings, but we can certainly make the most of the brief time that we have together. As the years speed by, it would be nice to know that we are creating warm memories to accompany the other trophies of a life half lived (like stretch marks, laugh lines, and a bottle of Grecian Formula in the shower stall).

Want to make sure you're making fond memories? Here are four ideas.

### *Tradition*

You don't have to repeat something twenty-seven times for it to become a cherished memory. Over the course of a child's eighteen years in your home, repeating something three to six times can actually elevate it to the status of a "tradition." I cherish the memory of my parents rousing my sisters and me in the middle of the night to drive to Bob's Big Boy for hot chocolate. In reality, how many times did this midnight madness occur? Probably only a handful. But looking back over my childhood, it stands out as a favorite memory.

## *Integration*

That means your life with theirs. There has to be some overlap or there will be no shared memories. I was moved by a recent article I read about athlete Bo Jackson. When he retired from professional baseball, he didn't cite as his reason advancing age or an injury or a contract dispute. Instead, he told a story about a conversation his wife had with their son. The youngster approached his mom and asked why Daddy was never home. She tried to explain, but it apparently wasn't to the child's satisfaction because, after a moment's thought, he posed another question. "Does Daddy have another family somewhere else?" Jackson concluded: "If that isn't enough for any man to make up his mind, then he isn't a man. And he isn't a father."

## *Motivation*

What is your motivation for spending time with your kids? I applaud the dad who, after a long day, makes the choice to override his overwhelming desire to flee to Mexico and instead steels himself and takes his children to Showbiz Pizza for some madhouse memory-making. Or the mother whose every nerve is screaming for Calgon as she tells her toddler through clenched jaws, "Of course I'll read *I'm a Bunny* one more time, Tommy." We've all experienced times when our desires don't have anything to do with playing Parent of the Year, and yet our commitment to our children wins out. Okay, so we may have to work a bit to convince our kids that we're actually having fun, but it's better than ignoring them altogether, isn't it?

Of course it is. Being motivated by commitment is a legitimate expression of your love. It takes some effort on your part, but it has the power to build the esteem of your children and deepen your relationship with them.

Unless . . .

Unless it's all they get.

To grow the best memories, our kids have to know that sometimes . . . every now and then . . . once a month or week or day . . . we are seeking out their company, not because we know we should, but because we just can't resist. They need to know that we are not merely committed, but crazy about them, that the routine of parenting has, at least for a few moments or hours, been transformed into a romance of sorts. We love our children . . . but are we in love with them? Do we enjoy their company? Relish their witty remarks? Cherish our time together? Are we encumbered or enamored? Is parenting a priority or a passion?

*To grow the best memories, our kids have to know that sometimes we are seeking out their company, not because we know we should, but because we just can't resist.*

If you're not sure, ask your kids. My guess is that they'll know the answers to these questions right away.

Our commitment to our kids helps us plod through some of life's more stressful or distracting seasons. Our unfettered joy at the privilege of raising them helps us soar. Both are necessary. To think that we can make it through our years of parenting with all passion and no plodding is unrealistic. To think that we can make it on sheer commitment and no romance is sad. Strike a balance. Your memories of your time together as a family will be richer as a result.

### *Elevation*

Finally, look for opportunities to elevate your child's esteem. Some of life's most powerful memories recall the way we felt at a certain time and place. Your child may not be able to remember the name of the hotel where your family stayed during a summer vacation, but she'll always remember how loved she felt when you took the time to help her spell her name in seashells on the beach. Look for opportunities to foster warm feelings rather than to merely put a checkmark by an activity "successfully completed." After all, even if we take the time to *do* things with our children, yet constantly nag and berate them during the process, we're sabotaging our efforts and undermining, rather than building, the relationship we share.

Want to make a memory? Remember the principles of . . .

**T**radition

**I**ntegration

**M**otivation and

**E**levation

Sure, it takes "time," but your investment today will reap dividends for decades to come.

## Preserving Memories

Maybe I feel a need to include this section because of my own tired memory. How tired is my memory? One of my greatest stresses in life is introducing one friend to another because I'm never quite sure that I'll remember both names. It doesn't matter who I'm introducing: I could be introducing my mother to my best friend and my blood pressure would go up.

How tired is my memory? Once I listened to a telemarketer for fifteen minutes because she greeted me by saying, "Hello, Mrs. Linamen, this is Carol Smith . . ." and it took me that long to conclude that, no, this was not a personal call from someone I knew but just couldn't place.

But at least I'm not alone on this journey toward senility. Yesterday one of my friends admitted that his memory, like mine, short circuits from time to time. Mike Talley's story went like this: He was driving to work one morning when he realized he had forgotten to brush his teeth. When he got to his office in a secured government building, he sent his brief-case through the metal detector. He was seated in his eighth-floor office before noticing he'd left his briefcase at the security station. While downstairs retrieving his briefcase, he walked into a lobby gift shop to buy some Dentyne (to cover his morning breath), and was back at his desk be-fore it dawned on him that he'd left his purchase next to the cash register. Is it any wonder the poor man had trouble finding his car when it was time to go home?

*How tired is my memory? Once I listened to a telemarketer for fifteen minutes because she greeted me by name and it took me that long to conclude that, no, this was not a personal call from someone I knew but just couldn't place.*

We are the NutraSweet generation, after all. Armed with our Day-Timers and electronic secretaries and beepers, we lull ourselves into believing that, no, we're not forgetting anything important. But let's face it! Life in the '90s is moving along at a clip that even Han Solo and Chewbacca blasting into hyperspace would have a hard time keeping up with.

Is it any wonder it's sometimes hard to recall the intimate details regarding high-lights and milestones of family life? If we go to all the "time" and effort to create warm memories with our families, can we be certain we'll remember them in the fall and winter of our lives? When did Junior lose his first tooth? What funny phrases were Jennifer's favorites as a baby? What intimate con-versations and Kodak moments have you experienced with your teenager that may have managed to slip your mind?

My ten-year-old asked me last week how old she was when she took her first steps and I told her, unequivocally and with a high degree of confidence, that it was at some point before she started kindergarten.

I don't mean to forget these things. I want to remember, really I do. Preserving these memories is important to me, as it no doubt is to you. How can we keep them from slipping away? Here are seven ideas.

## Keep a Diary

No, I'm not talking about spending an hour each night penning your deepest thoughts, fears, and fantasies. I'm talking about taking five minutes to jot down three highlights from your day. Did your son experience his first date? Was he nervous? Were you? Did your husband buy you flowers unexpectedly? Was this the date of the fortieth wedding anniversary party you planned for your parents and, if so, what do you most want to remember about the evening? Almost any kind of blank book, calendar, or daily planner will work for this kind of record. If daily jotting seems too much, take a few minutes once a week—every Sunday afternoon, or during your lunch hour one day a week—to record recent highlights. All told, it's not much effort, and you'll be glad in the long run that you took the time.

## Snapshots Paint the Picture

Carry your camera with you—to church, school plays, picnics, shopping trips, birthday parties, soccer events, family vacations—and click liberally. Film and developing charges are relatively cheap compared to the cost of restaging that family vacation to the Grand Canyon or, worse, realizing your family is grown and there's no going back to recapture the magic of their childhood on film. Some suggestions for family shutterbugs:

*Personalize travel pictures.* Face it, your shot of the Great Wall of China isn't going to compare with that fifty-cent postcard you can buy from a tourist stand and glue in your photo album . . . unless, of course, you personalize your snapshot with the people you love! Put your spouse or kids in the foreground. They can stand still and look cute, or you may want to stage some action. When we traveled to Greece, I wanted to create a fun snapshot contrasting old and new: Framing the majestic ruins of the Acropolis in the background, I plunked my six-year-old daughter in the foreground eating Gummi Worms.

*Take advantage of dramatic natural light.* The light at sunrise and sunset is a rich blend of exotic tones that can enhance any subject.

*Watch those toes!* Professionals and amateurs alike tend to leave too much headroom and slice people off at the ankles.

*Remember the rule of thirds.* Taking a picture of your daughter standing in a field of flowers? Don't place her dead center in your snapshot, but to the left or right of center. Imagine two vertical lines dissecting your viewfinder into three equal parts. Place the image of your daughter at one of those two lines. The same idea goes for horizon shots: Imagine two horizontal lines dividing your viewfinder into three segments. Place the horizon at one of these two lines so it is *not* perfectly centered between the top and bottom of your snapshot. This configuration can add interest and energy to your photos.

*Reduce red-eye.* Red eyes occur when your subject's pupils enlarge to accommodate a darkened, indoor setting, and then are reflected in the head-on glare of a camera flash. Some cameras have special flashes that can reduce those an-

*My ten-year-old asked me last week how old she was when she took her first steps and I told her, unequivocally and with a high degree of confidence, that it was at some point before she started kindergarten.*

noying red eyeballs by flashing twice—the first flash causes the pupil to shrink in response to the light. The second flash illuminates the scene for the photo. Some other techniques are:

Use a camera with a flash that perches on top of the camera, so your subject isn't looking point-blank at the light when it pops.

Make sure the room is well-lit so that pupils shrink, reducing red-eye.

Pose subjects so that they are not looking directly at the camera, but looking at each other, a flower, birthday present, or whatever.

Snap photos outside, in daylight.

*Protect your gear.* When traveling with camera equipment, consider hauling your things in something other than a camera bag, which might attract theft! Consider a diaper bag or even a small cooler. Also, don't rely on a towel or jacket to cover valuable equipment in the seat or on the floor of a locked car. That old towel trick can be a dead giveaway to thieves that something of value is only a broken window away!

### Create Themed Photo Albums

Chronological albums are great. But what about photobooks that document recurring events year after year after year? Make duplicates of photos from birthdays, Christmases, summer vacations, or the first day of each new school year and display them in an album devoted solely to that kind of event. It will be fun to view the changes in your family from year to year, for example, in a photo album devoted just to Christmas snapshots! You might even find other types of things to add to your theme scrapbook. Your Christmas photo album, for example, can also display your family's favorite holiday recipes, the letter to Santa your five-year-old wrote last year, or the annual Christmas letter from Grandma and Grandpa.

## Photo Boxes Save Memories and Time

If keeping up with photo albums and scrapbooks seems like a lot of trouble, don't stop snapping those pix! Each January label a photo box for that year. You can buy photo boxes at any variety store, or use a large shoe box with the year inked on the front end. Keep negatives in an envelope in the box, along with your photos for that year. (It helps if you keep them stacked chronologically, but even that isn't necessary!) There's no law that photos have to be stored in an album—the only crime would be if the dread of keeping an album kept you from capturing your memories on film.

## Corral School Art and Papers for Posterity

I don't know about your kids, but mine have radar that alerts them when any one of the 4,000 drawings and worksheets they bring home daily from school leaves my refrigerator and hits the trash. They want to save EVERYTHING. This not only clutters my home, it creates a fire hazard and, somewhere near the end of the school year, begins to hinder access to various rooms in our home.

Try this: Buy one cardboard file box for each child, to be used year after year. This is where every piece of artwork or schoolwork goes until the end of summer. At that point, have your child select twenty-five items to save from the pile. Save these items in a clean cardboard pizza box. (To obtain one, beg, borrow, or bribe with hard cash from your local pizzeria. I called three pizza stores about availability of boxes— local mom-and-pop establishments were more willing to give or sell me an unused box than the national chains.) The pizza boxes work nicely because they hold large pieces of artwork, and stack neatly on a closet shelf or beneath a bed!

### Video-Mania

The price of a video camera is small compared to what you get in return: the ability to revisit the past, and in living color, no less. Ivey Suber is a former videographer for CBS. Today he owns his own company—Unique Video Productions of Dallas—and produces videos for the sports, news, and entertainment industries and for the corporate world as well. He had these home-movie tips for moms and dads:

*Don't get zoom-happy.* The button is fun, but constant zooming in and out can be distracting to viewers. Use zooms sparingly.

*Steady does it.* When holding the camera, use both hands and lock your elbows to steady the picture. Lean against a wall or tree for added stability. And when possible, avoid handheld shots altogether, using a tripod for the steadiest shots.

> **When holding a video camera, use both hands and lock your elbows to steady the picture. Lean against a wall or tree for added stability.**

*Monitor your audio.* If you're recording sound, grab a simple headset (one from your Walkman will do) and plug it into the audio jack on your camera. This will enable you to hear the audio exactly as it is being recorded and to make adjustments as necessary.

*Edit with your camera.* When taping a scene, hold the camera as steady as possible. When the scene is over, turn the camera off. Don't resume taping until your next scene is focused and composed in the viewfinder. Too many people leave the tape running as they reframe, refocus, and transition from scene to scene. This not only wastes tape, but is distracting to viewers.

## Letters Tell the Story

If you are a letter writer, consider keeping copies of newsy letters that you write to family members and friends. Years from now, you'll enjoy rereading about your son's winning soccer play as you described it in a letter to Grandma.

Preserving family memories doesn't happen without effort, but the effort pays off in the end. That's because the time we spend today provides a rich link to the past, the people we've loved, and the laughter we've shared. No matter what Miss Clairol says, we *are* getting older, every one of us. The good news is that with every passing year, our collection of old memories and new ones gives us something more to cherish and remember.

### Preserving Fun Family Memories? Try these ideas:

- Keep a diary.
- Take lots of snapshots.
- Create themed photo albums.
- If photo albums seem too time-consuming, use photo boxes for a no-fuss way to store and preserve photos!

- Save school artwork and schoolwork in clean pizza boxes, which stack neatly beneath a bed.
- Invest in a video camera.
- If you're in the habit of writing newsy letters to relatives, make photocopies for yourself before you pop the letters in the mail.

## Myth #12

# You Can Work at Home and Earn $1,000 a Week

e've all seen the ads suggesting that, by working from the comfort of our own homes, we can pull in masses of money that would impress even Robin Leach.

If you've ever responded to one of these ads, like I have, you have discovered how the really big money is made: by selling mailing lists containing our names and addresses to every get-rich schemer and snake-oil salesman this side of River City!

I made one measly phone call to discover how I could make a million dollars without so much as stepping onto my front porch, and suddenly my mailbox has become a magnet for unsolicited fliers, postcards, letters, and audiotapes promising riches galore. The one person experiencing bet-

ter cash flow as a result of all this is my mailman: He's so mus-
cled from hefting all my junk mail that he's closed out his gym
membership, saving more than six hundred dollars a year.

Just yesterday I got a letter promising to help me turn my
"lunch money into millions!" To receive my start-up kit, all I have
to do is mail in a check for $69.99. Excuse me? Seventy dollars?
I don't know where *they* eat lunch, but when I think of "lunch
money" I think of Burger King on Dollar Wednesday.

I even get letters from financial psychics who will reveal
to me my lucky lotto number if I call *their* lucky number, which is 1-900-GET-
RICH, for only three dollars a minute.

*Can we convince the American public that dust bunnies make good pets? Or that chewing gum recycled from under the kitchen table is a viable adhesive for hanging pictures or repairing household items?*

And I can't even enumerate all the
correspondence I've gotten from lawyers
who have found a way to make pyramid
letters PERFECTLY LEGAL, thus raking
in millions of dollars and financing an
early retirement to a beach bungalow in
the Cayman Islands, which is why they
can't be reached for comment. I am assured, in these letters, that my suspicions
should not be aroused by the fact that
the lawyer cannot reveal his name to me,
or that the mimeographed letter is rid-
dled with typos, or even that the postage
stamp was canceled in a little town just
outside of Folton State Prison. All I need
to know is that this money-making
scheme is PERFECTLY LEGAL. That, and
the name of a good lawyer.

### Financing Family Life

You know, we don't really need millions, do we? Most of
us would be happy with a little extra money at the end of the
month. Or maybe a little less month at the end of our bud-

gets. Personally, I'd like to see the institution of a three-week month. That would make a big difference right there.

It doesn't matter if we live in a mansion or a trailer, have no children or five, bring home double or single incomes, make lots of dough or merely peanuts. Every family could use a little extra money.

How can we improve our cash flow? Basically, we have two options. We can make more money. Or we can spend less. Let's start by taking a look at making more money:

## Create a Market, Make a Mint

I am convinced that you and I are sitting on financial gold mines. We don't need to leave our homes in order to make lots of money, because our homes are the very things that can provide us with financial independence. This is because family life provides a virtually limitless supply of many—let's see, how should I say this—*products* that can be parlayed into big bucks for innovative families. All we have to do is create a market for these items, and you and I will never have to clip coupons again.

The question is, can we do it? Can we convince the American public that dust bunnies make good pets? Or that chewing gum recycled from under the kitchen table is a viable adhesive for hanging pictures or repairing household items? And what about those Bounce dryer sheets? Once the fabric softener is gone, wouldn't they make great tissue stuffing for gift bags?

Maybe we could market empty toilet paper rolls as holders for loose lamp cords. Or the aluminum lids from cans of frozen orange juice as coasters.

And what about Barbie wigs made out of used Brillo pads? Think about it! Our motto could be "Give Barbie a Bad Hair Day!" Moms everywhere would flock to buy these things. We could go on to offer stick-on stretch marks and crows' feet to give the plastic dream doll an even bigger dose of reality.

Mateless socks provide yet another generous source for an innovative product, and I've got just the right marketing idea. Last Christmas, I filled a sock with uncooked rice, sealing the opening with a knot. I tied a girl's hair ribbon around the knot to give the impression of a ponytail, then used permanent markers to draw a picture of a face on the sock. I dubbed my creation "Miss Cozette," then penned the following instructions for an adult white elephant gift that proved to be the toast of our Sunday school class Christmas party:

Make Miss Cozette
Your Bedtime Buddy!

Put Miss Cozette in the microwave for three
to four minutes (don't let her get overheated)
and then pop her under the covers for a
toasty time. She'll heat you
up for half an hour or more (which is more
than can be said for many spouses).

Contents: Rice, Sock (may or may not have been worn).

Imagine the income! We could harvest products from junk drawers and kids' rooms and bulging closets. We could create our sales catalog from what we discover beneath sofas and on the floors of family vans. And as long as we have children in our homes, we would have a never-ending supply of raw materials with which to operate. Our overhead would be practically nonexistent! We'd be millionaires within months! Our financial problems would be over!

We could afford new HOMES and drive new CARS.

We could even join expensive spas. In no time at all, we'd have *thin thighs* AND whiter teeth, and our husbands would all start to look like TOM SELLECK! Our lives would be perfect! Our kids would never forget to put the new roll of toilet paper on the spindle, WE WOULD NEVER PUT ANOTHER PAIR OF PANTY HOSE ON CROOKED, and scientists would discover that eating chocolate in large quantities can prevent PMS, enhance sex, and reduce the national debt!

*"Most get-rich-quick opportunities don't work. Most people who actually make the big bucks are doing something they love or have a special talent for doing."*

On second thought . . .

If our lives were too perfect, we'd go bankrupt. This is because the perfect life does not include dust bunnies beneath the couch, chewed gum under the kitchen table, or socks without mates. Rusty Brillo pads would no longer enjoy long lives next to the bottles of dish soap on our kitchen sinks. And perfectly good empty toilet paper rolls would be placed in the trash by responsible and well-mannered children, instead of spending weeks on the bathroom spindle where we could find them when we needed them.

And then what would happen to our entrepreneurial enterprises?

Oh well. It was a nice dream while it lasted.

## You Can Work from Home . . . and Make Enough

Maybe making millions from my living room is unlikely. But what about making a respectable living, earning a little spending money, or supplementing a savings account? Is it possible for moms (and dads) to work at home and meet these kinds of goals?

A growing number of people are saying yes. What are some of the professions setting up shop between the laundry room and the family TV? Child care, secretarial services, legal services, writing and graphic arts, and even database consulting are a few of the many choices.

According to one woman who works from home, selecting the right business means focusing on your skills and passions, rather than looking for easy dollars in an unfamiliar field: "When looking for a business to run from home, don't look for an opportunity that promises lots of money. Look for something that you enjoy or are good at, and then find a way to make money at it. Most get-rich-quick opportunities don't work. Most people who actually make the big bucks are doing something they love or have a special talent for doing."

*My husband understands that Fannie Mae does not sell fruit cobblers in the frozen foods section of our grocery store.*

Two excellent resources designed to help women find their niche are the books entitled *101 Best Home-Based Businesses for Women* (1995) and *101 Best Small Businesses for Women* (1996), published by Prima Publishing in Rocklin, California. Author Priscilla Huff examines such practical stuff as start-up costs, how and where to advertise, essential equipment, what to charge for your services, income potential, and where to find your best customers. They are great choices if you're looking for road-tested insights from someone who's been where you want to go!

## A Penny Saved Is a Penny Earned

Earning more money is one way to boost cash flow. Another way is to spend less of what you have. But, of course, I'm writing on hearsay, having never actually engaged in the fine art of saving money. At least not intentionally. Several months ago I was surprised to pull, from my washing machine, a five dollar bill left over from the previous month's budget, but I would have spent it sooner if I'd known where it was, so I don't think this counts.

Much to my husband's chagrin and dismay, I'm not a saver. Oh, I can save things like junk mail, loose buttons, and tuna casserole that's been in the refrigerator since October. And saving resources is okay, too: I would love to launch a public service campaign that says, "Conserve water—wash your dishes once a week," or "Conserve energy—yours!—and hire a maid!"

But cash . . . well, that's another story. Luckily, my husband is a good financial planner. He's got IRAs and KEOGHs and 403-Bs. He understands that Fannie Mae does not sell fruit cobblers in the frozen foods section of our grocery store. He even keeps a running total in his check register. And when he opens a savings account, it has nothing to do with wanting overdraft protection in case he bounces a check.

Saving money comes more naturally to some people than others. But even for those of us who think losing ten pounds is easier than saving ten dollars, it pays to learn to save. How can saving money reap dividends for our families?

- Better cash flow is a definite plus. A savings account provides a financial buffer to help us cope with unexpected emergencies and even afford a few luxuries now and then.

- Feeling financially "in control" can help us feel more confident and "in charge" in *every* area of our lives. I know that, for me, self-discipline is contagious—when I have any one area of my life "together," I sometimes have more confidence and energy available to help me stay on top of other areas, such as diet, exercise, or housework.

- The careful management of your money can make the difference between needing two incomes or one. In fact, with some financial savvy, it may be possible for you to live more comfortably on one income than many families with less money-smarts can live on two.

## Want to Save Money? Ask the Experts

How can we become better savers? There are lots of great books on the market that have to do with saving money. Two of my favorites are *The Tightwad Gazette I* and *II* by Amy Dacyczyn.

Amy began her quest toward self-proclaimed "tightwaddery" several years into her marriage. Hoping to stay home full-time with her children, she set out to prove wrong naysayers who warned her that double incomes are a must-have for families today. Rather than supplementing her husband's salary with her own career (or answering the ads promising Fast Cash for Work-at-Home Folks), she went about the task of saving every conceivable dollar in order to live successfully on one income.

Amy offers a lot of fun tips and some weird ones as well. I'm not particularly interested, for example, in using dryer lint to make a "lint mâché" Halloween mask for my children, or recycling used shower curtains into baby bibs, or making a jump rope from plastic bread bags and duct tape.

Nevertheless, the books offer plenty of sound advice. This is how I learned that I can extend the life of windshield wiper blades by cleaning them with vinegar and water . . . that cooking food in my microwave costs five times less than using my electric oven . . . that chewing gum and duct tape can help me avoid a costly plumber's bill . . . and that tracking the price of grocery staples at various stores can yield some surprising information and help me save big on my weekly supermarket bill. (I followed Amy's *Supermarket Price Book* advice and discovered that for the past four years I'd been shopping at a store that is, consistently, 50 cents to one dollar higher *per item*. Yikes!)

## Whose Dollars Are These, Anyway?

There is no shortage of creative strategies to help determined families save a buck. Yet despite the proliferation of money-saving tips, books, seminars, and products available to our families, saving money successfully seems to boil down to being able to master and put into daily practice a single skill:

Spending less.

Easier said than done, I know.

One thing that is helping me is a change of perspective.

Recently Toby Snowden, pastor of High Pointe Baptist Church where we attend, spoke from the pulpit about resources. And something that he said stuck with me.

He said that my money belongs to God.

I know, we've all heard that before. But he really got me thinking. What if I took that concept to heart? What if it penetrated not only my heart, but my checkbook as well? What if I considered myself accountable to God for every dollar of his that I spend?

"Hey, God, I need milk and diapers for my kids. I know you want my children to be cared for—is this a good use of your money? I thought so, too."

"Hey, God, there's this movie we've been wanting to see. It's rated PG (just in case you were wondering). It may seem frivolous, but Larry and I have really been needing some time away, just the two of us, and I know that rest, relaxation, and fun are part of your will for our lives! Can I have ten bucks of your money to use toward that end? What? Take twenty and have dinner, too? Thanks!"

"Hey, God, Kaitlyn and Kacie need new shoes—again. Thank you for healthy, growing girls, but couldn't you have come up with a better system for maturing young feet? Instead of making feet grow slow but steady, couldn't you make them stay the same shape for several years . . . and then jump two sizes overnight? I could save so much . . . What? Stop complaining and get over to Payless Shoes? Two for one sale? No kidding! Thanks for the tip. Oh yeah, and thanks for the money. I know this is coming out of your pocket, not mine."

Sound silly? Maybe. Of course, no one has time to pray over every box of macaroni and cheese, or every dry cleaning receipt, or every McDonald's hamburger.

But there's something to be said for daily remembering whose money we're spending and asking for wisdom in how we spend it.

When I am functioning in this mode, three things tend to happen.

First, I have fewer bouts of impulse spending. Do you know when I tend to spend crazy and end up with a bad case of the budget blues? When I am emotionally and spiritually out of kilter. When I am angry or depressed or overwhelmed, I make less-than-stellar financial decisions. The interesting thing is that, when I am in these kinds of moods, I'm usually not feeling very spiritual. Approaching God in prayer doesn't feel particularly comfortable. If I consider praying about a purchase—and realize that I don't really WANT to pray—it may be a good sign that I am not in any condition to make wise financial decisions and would probably do well to stay out of the mall until I can adjust my attitude.

Do I have to "hear" from God and "wait upon him" for an answer every time I want to spend a dollar? Not really. In fact, many times I can learn most of what I need to know by evaluating my willingness to pray. If my heart is in sync with God's, there's a good chance my spending will be, too.

Second, I am less likely to skimp on tithing. The Bible states clearly that we are to give the first fruits of our labor back to the God who provides for us so adequately in the first place. In terms of money, that means ten percent of what we earn. The other request that is made of us is that we do this with a glad heart.

Yikes. When I perceive my resources as belonging to me, me, me, I have a hard time doing this. I think about the bills I've got and the expenses coming up, and I know I'm going to need every last dollar (and then some) to stay out of the red. Give money to God? Give MY money to God? I guess . . .

if I HAVE to . . . I want to be obedient, but . . . ouch. Couldn't he be happy with an IOU instead?

When I think, however, of my money as God's rather than mine, tithing makes a lot more sense. If it's not mine to begin with, it's a lot easier to let go of on Sunday morning when the offering plate comes around.

Third, I experience no small amount of peace, knowing that if my assets belong to God, so do my liabilities! Do I still worry about money? Sure. Do I still fret over finances? You bet. But if I'm making an effort to spend wisely, and I'm also being obedient by tithing with a cheerful heart, then it's a lot easier to turn my finances over to my Father and say, "Here, Dad, ultimately this is your responsibility. You are my provision in every area. I'm doing all I can to do right in this area, and I'm trusting you to take care of me."

*There's something to be said for daily remembering whose money we're spending and asking for wisdom in how we spend it.*

What happens when you view your money as belonging to God's pocketbook and not your own? I believe you'll experience more wisdom in your spending . . . you'll find new joy in tithing . . . and you'll have greater peace about your financial future—dividends that would make any banker proud!

 **Don't Get Taken by a Fast-Cash Scam!**

Priscilla Huff tells us how to avoid fast cash scams. For additional information visit her web site:
http://www.webbrokers.com/215453/littlehouse

With the rapid growth in the home-based movement has come a growth in fraudulent money-making schemes. Pick up any newspaper or magazine and you will see advertisements that offer work-at-home opportunities—reading books, assembling crafts, sewing baby items, stuffing envelopes—or information on starting a business related to medical claims, travel, computers, and more.

Many of these schemes have a toll-free number; however, most will then ask you for money for additional information. They may promise that you will make thousands of dollars a month working from your kitchen table. They may even offer a computer and special business software and personnel you can call to help you get your business going. Sounds too good to be true, doesn't it? It often is!

One older couple I know went with a company like this and borrowed $15,000 on their home to purchase the computer and software required. The computer and software turned out to be outdated—but the real problem was that they did not know how to market the business opportunities they purchased. This couple would have been better off to have spent some time researching the market in their community, and used that $15,000 toward starting their own little successful business doing something in which they already may have had experience, and with a potential customer base.

When looking for ways to make money from your home, avoid any business opportunity that does the following:

- Promises huge profits in your spare time
- Asks for money before they send you any of the business details
- Refuses to give you the names of others who have invested in this business opportunity
- Requests money for work-at-home resources

158

## Want to Save Money? Four Ways to Save Big

1. Keep track of what you have. It seems downright silly to reuse aluminum foil to save a few cents when record-keeping mayhem results in bounced-check charges, late fees, and finance charges adding up to much bigger money. A single returned check, for example, can mean $25 to your bank and $25 to the vendor. Forgetting to pay bills on time can mean late fees of five, ten, or even fifty bucks per bill! Careful record-keeping can add up to significant savings in the long run.

2. Pay off credit card debt. It's estimated that the average American family owes $2,500 in credit card debt and pays nearly $500 annually in finance charges. Want to save big? Nix the plastic. Consider cutting up cards until your balance is paid off. Then, if you choose to keep your cards, charge only what you can afford, paying off your balance in full each month and keeping your running balance at zero.

3. Don't speed while driving. Driving within the speed limit conserves fuel and saves money at the gas pump. But there's bigger savings to be realized: A single speeding ticket can cost hundreds of dollars when you calculate the cost of the fine plus higher insurance premiums.

4. Pay off your mortgage in fifteen years instead of thirty. When Larry and I chose this option, we increased our monthly mortgage by $100, from $950 to $1,050. A similar way we could have reached our goal would have been to make one extra payment annually, paying $950 thirteen times each calendar year instead of twelve.

This means fifteen extra payments over the course of fifteen years (a grand total of less than $15,000). And yet doing this means we will avoid twelve payments each year for fifteen additional years (more than $170,000!).

159

To shorten an existing loan, check with your mortgage company to make sure there are no prepayment penalties; then begin this month increasing your payment by ten percent. A small sacrifice for a season will reap monster savings over the long haul!

# M&M's Melt in Your Mouth, Not in Your Hand

e've all watched enough TV to know that M&M's melt in your mouth, not in your hand. Of course, any mother who has discovered her child eating M&M's in the same room with her brand-new sofa will tell you that this slogan is nothing but a meanspirited joke.

Maybe this is because children know how to get around all the rules. The fact is that, held long enough in a hot chubby hand, an M&M will not only melt, it will melt with vigor and passion. It's possible that advertising executives don't know this because they themselves have never clutched an M&M for the amount of time it takes for this to happen. Children, however, do this by instinct.

> **What mother wouldn't appreciate a disclaimer printed on a cereal box that just came right out and admitted, "This cereal is primarily food coloring and sugar. Regular use of this product will have your dentist driving a Jaguar inside of a year"?**

In my opinion, the only reason Timex watches take a licking and keep on ticking is because they're worn and abused by adults, not children. And I am thoroughly convinced that Samsonite TV ads feature primates manhandling their luggage because a gorilla is far easier on a suitcase than a fifteen-year-old could ever be.

Don't you wish advertisers would just be honest with us? It would be nice to be told, for example, that the new toy I'm thinking about purchasing for an amount of money roughly equivalent to last month's rent will keep my toddler happy and entertained for all of twenty minutes, or until she discovers the box the toy came in, whichever comes first.

It would be helpful to know that the real reason so many toys say "Not intended for children under three" is not because the toy would be dangerous to a toddler, but because a two-year-old could turn that poorly constructed toy into garden mulch faster than you could say "Snuffle-upagus."

And what mother wouldn't appreciate a disclaimer printed somewhere on a cereal box that just came right out and admitted, "This cereal is primarily food coloring and sugar. Regular use of this product will have your dentist driving a Jaguar inside of a year"?

The world is full of catchy slogans and pretty promises. But what happens when ad hype meets real life? For years, advertisers have been promising us the moon in exchange for a few of our hard-earned dollars. But can they be trusted? Are we really choosier mothers if we buy Jif? Can Calgon really take us away? Can Dentyne honestly get our husbands to kiss us a little longer?

## Better Living through Consumerism

I'm a sucker for a good commercial. It doesn't matter if I'm in the market for a product or not—I'm drawn to commercials I think are clever or even quirky.

One of my favorites used to be the Bartles and Jaymes commercials featuring Frank Bartles and Ed Jaymes. If you never saw the ads, picture Iowa farmhands peddling wine coolers.

One day I was in the supermarket when I spied a pyramid of Bartles and Jaymes behind a lifesized poster of Frank and Ed. I remember looking at the price and thinking, "That seems reasonable." The next thing I knew I was wheeling my grocery cart toward Frank Bartles himself.

I came to my senses halfway across the aisle.

I don't drink alcohol.

It was a startling moment, to say the least.

*Let me just say that advertising directors don't spend billions of dollars annually on TV commercials so that station managers will send them fruitcake at Christmas.*

Oh, the power of television. We think we're immune to its charms. We tell ourselves that our wants, desires, and values aren't shaped by what we see when we gaze hypnotically into its glowing red eye.

We're wrong, of course.

The media has a huge impact on our lives. How much of an impact? Let me just say that advertising directors don't spend billions of dollars annually on TV commercials so that station managers will send them fruitcake at Christmas. No, they spend those kinds of dollars because they are getting even more dollars in return. Whose dollars? Ours.

I don't mean to bash the marketing industry. In fact, my first job out of college was writing catalog copy for a company that marketed, among other things, plastic glow-in-the-dark nativity sets. Even today, when I'm not writing books, I write marketing and public relations copy for several clients. I believe in marketing. It's good. It's effective. And it's the only way I know to pull in twenty-five bucks an hour (I mean legally).

> *I'm dreading the day I'll be watching TV and a product spokesperson informs me that there are only 364 more shopping days till Christmas.*

But that doesn't mean that marketers don't go overboard. And it certainly doesn't mean we have to believe everything we're told. And it REALLY doesn't mean that we actually NEED every product on the market today.

Day after day, we're subjected to the message that we can experience better living though consumerism. We can look better, feel better, smell better . . . we can have whiter teeth and smaller hips and shinier hair . . . we can be more productive, have more friends, and make more money . . .

. . . and all we have to do is spend $19.95 for one wonder product or another.

## Only 364 More Shopping Days till Christmas

Remember when we were kids and the Christmas shopping mania didn't begin until after Thanksgiving? Those were the good ol' days. This year, about the time the Christmas fliers started showing up in my mailbox, our postman was still wearing shorts. I spotted my first Santa while driving home after buying sparklers from a fireworks stand. What's worse, he had a tan.

It's hard to think about shopping for Christmas when the thing you put on before leaving for the mall is not your coat and gloves, but sunscreen and mosquito repellent.

I'm dreading the day I'll be watching TV and a product spokesperson informs me that there are only 364 more shopping days till Christmas. On second thought, at least it would still be cold outside . . .

Spend, spend, spend. And what do we get in return? Happiness, joy, and love? Try bills, bills, bills.

Some friends of ours tried a different approach this Christmas. Chris and Cami are the parents of four boys, three to twelve years of age. Instead of going into debt over Power Rangers and rollerblades, they told the boys the Christmas present they were going to receive this year was time.

Chris and Cami took a portion of what they normally spend on gifts and bought a collection of card games, board games, party games, and puzzles. The family spent Christmas vacation huddled around the kitchen table amassing monopolies, scrabbling for words, puzzling over puzzles, and searching for clues regarding the whereabouts of Miss Peacock and Colonel Mustard.

One week, two bags of popcorn, and 112 cups of hot chocolate later, Chris and Cami say it was one of the most enjoyable holidays they can remember.

Better living through consumerism? I don't think so. If you want to improve your life, don't reach for your wallet. Reach for the people you love instead. Spend time. Share a laugh. Make a memory. Get a life.

## Learning to Be Content with What We Have

In my book *The Parent Warrior* I tell about an incident that took place when Kaitlyn was about six years old. My mom and sister Michelle had flown into town for a visit, and one afternoon we four "girls" got all dressed up and drove to the Lady Primrose, an antique shop and tearoom located in the Crescent Hotel in downtown Dallas.

The tearoom provides an extravaganza for the senses, brimming with rich color and soothing melody, subtle fragrance, and lots of good things to eat and drink.

Surrounded by Tiffany lamps, prints of English gardens, sprigs of ivy, and dusty volumes of Charles Dickens, we drank berry tea from whimsical rosebud teacups and caught up on the details of each other's lives. Even Kaitlyn, dressed in a floral dress and white gloves, had a story to share. She'd heard it in Sunday school and recited it with great enthusiasm, thrilled to be telling a story just like the grown-ups. It was a "learn from my mistake" kind of story about our youth pastor and how, rather than being thankful for the beat-up car he owned, he drove every day past a car lot and coveted the new cars. Kaitlyn said it just like that—"coveted"—and my mother, sister, and I smiled at how grown-up she sounded as she repeated the story verbatim.

After feasting on scones, cucumber sandwiches, and dainty chocolates, we left our table to browse the treasures of the tearoom. One corner in particular held Kaitlyn's attention. It was, of course, the nook filled with dolls and bears and picture books. Child-sized Queen Anne furniture beckoned from every direction. Dainty tea sets invited company. Beatrix Potter books and prints adorned tables and walls.

Kaitlyn was enthralled. I was in the process of deflecting a barrage of questions beginning with the words "Mama, can I *please* have . . ." when suddenly she stopped. Her hand still in mine, Kaitlyn looked up at me, an expression of surprise on her face.

"Mama," she whispered, "I think I'm coveting this room."

A small insight. A spiritual truth. It began as a story heard in Sunday school, and yet it held the seed of revelation for my six-year-old. Seeing her standing there, jam on her collar and surprise in her eyes, I wanted to laugh. And I wanted to cry.

Honestly, nothing prepares you for the rush of joy and gratitude that comes from seeing your children grasp an idea, a principle, a concept that will help them navigate life's wild waters. What a wonderful truth Kaitlyn grabbed hold of—if only for a few minutes—as she stood saucer-eyed in the midst of a fantasy world of exquisite possessions and things. You know, most of us adults haven't nailed down the concepts of being thankful for what we have and not coveting things we don't have. The fact that Kaitlyn, at six years old, could acknowledge these principles left me moved and humbled.

*It's true that my kids have bought into the idea that more is better. But so have I, and I'm the grown-up. I'm supposed to know better.*

Of course, learning the great truths of life is nothing less than a process. It takes time. And maturity. And mistakes. And many, many reminders along the way. Kaitlyn is ten, and she's still working on learning how to be content with what she has without always wanting more. (Frankly, I'm still trying to figure that one out for myself!)

When we go into a store together, I warn that she can ask the question "Mom, can I please have . . ." one time only. The only other rule is that she has to complete the sentence by naming one product, rather than by inserting the words "everything on aisle seven" or something equally as inclusive.

I have to set limits like this or the requests quickly exceed the sum total of our annual income. Luckily, Kacie is not yet at the stage where she asks to own everything in the entire store—she merely climbs out of the cart and plays hide-and-seek in the aisles and destroys merchandise, which means that she is actually the easier shopping partner.

Truthfully, I can handle Kaitlyn's unreasonable requests and out-of-control material desires. The more difficult challenge is me. It's true that my kids have bought into the idea that more is better. But so have I, and I'm the grown-up. I'm supposed to know better.

I asked my friend Cherie how we can teach our children— and ourselves as well—to be satisfied with what we have without always wanting more.

"You mean without selling the TV, becoming hermits, and living in a commune? You mean other than that?" she asked.

"Yes. Other than that."

## Just Say No

Perhaps the first resource available to parents is a single word: No.

"Can I have . . ."

No.

"Will you buy . . ."

No.

Of course, there are variations to this technique. One variation is the "No-plus-explanation" option, as in "No, you can't have a $17,000 sports car because I am neither brain-dead nor am I married to Donald Trump."

Another option is the "No-plus-character-building-alternative" approach in which you agree to let your child have the item in question if she agrees to earn the money for it herself.

Sometimes none of these techniques will stem the torrent of pleading coming from the lips of your child. You know this is happening when you have heard the same request in varying forms more than two dozen times. When placed in these circumstances, I have been known to ask my daughter a single question in my calmest and most rational voice: "I have just said no twenty-six times, and I'm a little curious about something: How many more times do you intend to ask me the exact same question? It's not that I mind, but I'm trying to plan out the rest of my afternoon and I'd like to know how many more times I'm going to need to tell you no."

Sometimes this actually works.

If not, I have been known to eventually resort to something called "The Broken Record Technique." Defined by Manuel J. Smith in his book *When I Say No, I Feel Guilty,* this technique can be used to deflect undue pressure being applied by anyone: a child, coworker, PTA chairperson . . . even a used-car salesman. The technique works because, instead of getting caught in a never-ending cycle of trying to defend your reasons, you state your final answer, then repeat it verbatim as many times as necessary:

"No, Trevor, I will not buy you a hundred-and-twenty-dollar pair of sneakers. I understand your disappointment, but I've explained my reasons and my answer will not change."

"But, Mom, blah blah blah blah . . ."

"No, Trevor, I will not buy you a hundred-and-twenty-dollar pair of sneakers. I understand your disappointment, but I've explained my reasons and my answer will not change."

"But I promise to blah blah blah blah . . ."

"No, Trevor, I will not buy you a hundred-and-twenty-dollar pair of sneakers. I understand your disappointment, but I've explained my reasons and my answer will not change."

"What if blah blah blah blah . . ."

"No, Trevor . . ."

You get the idea. Eventually Trevor will too.


## Set an Example

We can say no to our children's frivolous requests. We can explain our reasons. We can pontificate about the evils of materialism. We can discuss the difference between a "need" and a "want." And if none of that works, we can show them the balance in our checkbooks!

But we'll never truly convince them to be content with what they have unless we're willing to practice what we preach.

Earlier I quoted Cherie Spurlock about resorting to communal living as a way to teach kids to be content. But that's not all she had to say. She had a lot to say about letting our own values set the example for our families: "Like it or not, our kids learn from us. If they see that we're excited about staying home and playing a game instead of going to a movie, or about clothes without a designer label, then that's going to help shape their values, too. If we would like to have a better car, do we complain about what we have? Or do we talk about how grateful we are for what we have, even if it is a 1982 Nissan with a hundred and fifty thousand miles on it? When it comes to teaching our kids to be content, we have to practice what we preach."

> **Life doesn't "owe" us a steady stream of luxuries delivered to our front door.**

Of course, this comes about as naturally as losing those unwanted postnatal pounds. So Cherie and I came up with a few suggestions for the parent who wants to maintain a balanced perspective about materialism and pass that perspective on to her children.

1. *Focus on things that have eternal value rather than fleeting attraction.* One of the very best ways to maintain a good perspective on what is eternal is to acquaint ourselves with God's thoughts on the matter. In fact, we don't even have to be mind readers to know his perspective. This is because we have his very words recorded for us in the Bible. Read God's Word. Memorize it. The pages of your Bible have a lot to say about money, possessions, and priorities.

Like what? Hebrews 13:5 tells us to keep our lives free from the love of money and be content with what we have because

God has promised us that he will never leave us nor forsake us. In other words, God is enough. We can be content because he's all that we need.

First Timothy 6:6 promises that godliness with contentment is great gain. This is because we brought nothing into the world, and we can take nothing out of it. If we have food and clothing we can be content—it is enough.

And in Philippians 4:11 and 12, Paul says that he has learned the secret of being content in any and every situation, whether he is well fed or hungry, rich or poor. The secret: "I can do everything through him [Jesus Christ] who gives me strength" (verse 13).

Read your Bible. Let God's Word shape your attitude.

2. *Give to others who are in need.* Do you want to convince your kids that there's no truth to the bumper sticker that promises that "he who dies with the most toys, wins"? Then show them that life isn't about hoarding and accumulation. Give some of your stuff away. Give some of your time away. And most importantly, give some of your money away. You can tell your kids that it's better to give than receive. You can even make them share their things with others. But until they see you reaching into your own back pocket, they're not going to believe it for a minute.

3. *Take care of what you have.* Remember the old saying "Waste not, want not"? This may seem hard to swallow living in an age where everything is disposable and convenience is king. Nevertheless, when we take good care of the possessions with which we've been entrusted—our homes and cars, paychecks, clothes, and more—we're reminding ourselves and our kids that the accumulation of nice things is a privilege, not an inalienable right. Life doesn't "owe" us a steady stream of luxuries delivered to our front door. As for the nice things that come our way, they may be ours to enjoy, but they are also ours to maintain and to appreciate. Practice good stewardship of the good things in life.

With all the pressure on our families to have more . . . buy more . . . spend more . . . it's altogether too easy to develop an insatiable appetite for the things of this world. The bad news is that the love of possessions is a harsh master.

The good news is that we can choose whom we are going to serve.

Begin by making the right choice for yourself. Your kids are watching. Live the life you want them to emulate.

## Keeping Materialism in Check

How can we keep our families from buying into a mind-set that "more is better"? Here are some ideas:

- Kids love games. They also like gadgets. At the grocery store, provide your child with a calculator and let her figure which brand or size is the most economical. To determine cents per ounce, divide the product's price by the ounces. You might be surprised. Sometimes smaller quantities are more economical than mongo-packaging. And name-brands on sale are sometimes a better bargain than generics!
- Expose your child to various standards of living. Bake cookies for an elderly friend whose social security check affords few luxuries. Invite furloughed missionaries to spend an evening at your home, sharing stories and photo albums depicting the third world country where they've been living. Spend a Saturday morning volunteering at a soup kitchen. Drive through a disadvantaged neighborhood. Help your child grow into the awareness that while some families enjoy more luxuries than yours does, many fam-

ilies enjoy much less. There is no single living standard that is our "right" as Americans. The nice things that come our way need to be appreciated and taken care of.

- Practice generosity with your resources. Do you know someone with a financial need? Consider making a cash gift of fifty dollars, a hundred dollars, or more; then ask your kids to design a card to accompany the gift. Know any college students far from home? Invite them to join your family for Thanksgiving dinner, Saturday night tacos, or Easter brunch. The next time your church hosts a food drive, let your kids help you prepare a bag of groceries to donate. We think of "cash flow" as the relationship between family income and expenses. At your home practice the idea of "rivers of blessing." Don't collect your blessings in a stagnant pool with no outlet; instead, let a portion of your blessings flow through your home and into the lives of others—you'll be doubly blessed in the process!

# You, Too, Can Be a Superwoman

re you a real superwoman? Is your life in balance and in control? As you negotiate the dance between family and friends and work and self, do other women look at you and shake their heads in amazement and admiration?

Do you have the energy to remove your makeup and complete your entire skin-care regimen each and every night? Is there fresh baking soda in your refrigerator? Does your husband go to work each morning still smiling from the passion play the night before?

My guess is that, like me, you're no superwoman. In fact, if you're really like me, you don't even *know* any superwomen.

And yet we're so hard on ourselves, aren't we? We begin with such high expectations . . . and are dismayed to discover how short we fall.

## Superwoman, Go Home

Last week my friend Nancy was sitting in my den thumbing through the December issue of *Good Housekeeping* when she suddenly announced: "Doesn't it make you sick?"

"You mean the fact that our houses don't look like the ones in the magazines?" I asked.

"No, that they think women actually have the time to make all these holiday crafts and fancy recipes. The pictures look good, but no one really has the time for this."

I agree. I don't even have time to wash my hair *and* shave my legs during the same shower, much less design my own Christmas cards out of homemade paper or create a chocolate torte capable of moving Julia Childs to tears. Of course, that doesn't stop me from gazing longingly, even lustfully, at the pictures and fantasizing about the day when I might achieve full superwoman status.

Of all people, you'd think I would know better. After all, Linda Holland and I wrote about superwomen in our book *Working Women, Workable Lives.* We did a pretty good job, in fact, of smashing the myth that real, flesh-and-blood women can live up to superhuman expectations.

Even fantasy superheroes—you know, the ones who live entirely in comic books or on the silver screen—fall short of perfection. They have bad days. They even get whooped now and then.

Remember the Superman trilogy starring Christopher Reeves? One movie in particular stands out in my mind. For three-quarters of the show, our handsome hero manages to report the news, save the world, and woo the girl without breaking into a sweat. He corks a volcano, rounds up nuclear missiles in space, addresses the United Nations—and his curl never unfurls.

But after a grueling battle with a solar-powered nemesis, Superman retreats to nurse his wounds. Lois Lane finds him in his Clark Kent apartment, shivering beneath a blanket in a darkened room. Pale, weak, and drenched with fevered sweat, our hero is dying.

Even Superman has his limits.

In the movie, the comic-book hero recuperates and goes on to save the world—again. But real life isn't like that, is it? In real life, you and I don't get to reap the benefits of retakes and editing and stunt doubles and makeup artists who can work miracles. Our lives aren't scripted by professionals and no one is standing by with a special-effects crew when we try to leap tall buildings in a single bound.

*I don't even have time to wash my hair and shave my legs during the same shower, much less design my own Christmas cards out of homemade paper or create a chocolate torte capable of moving Julia Childs to tears.*

I know all this. I really do.

And yet I still have these really crazy expectations for myself. I still try to do it all, be it all, have it all. I keep thinking I can fly.

At these moments, it's good for me to try to get a grip on reality. I try to remind myself that, while I may be a superwoman wannabe, I'll never be a real superwoman. How do I know?

A real superwoman would never have to explain to her husband that the reason he hears his electric shaver going while he's still in bed every morning is because she's got these five REALLY persistent chin hairs . . .

A real superwoman would never be rushing to get ready for an important job interview, nick her leg shaving, and have to walk out the door wearing a Muppet Babies Band-Aid under her hose.

A real superwoman would never have to go on a diet. And if she did have to go on a diet, she would never cheat. And if she did happen to cheat, it would be for something rich and sophisticated, like caviar or chocolate mousse. She would never blow her diet because of an insatiable craving for Moon Pies or SweeTarts.

A real superwoman would never remove the tags that say DO NOT REMOVE from her pillows. And if she did remove them, she would do so with finesse and confidence. She would never lie awake at night wondering why she wasn't sup-posed to remove them, and what would happen to her if anybody found out.

*A real superwoman would not be growing eleven different strains of penicillin in her refrigerator.*

A real superwoman wouldn't tell her kids to save dinner leftovers in a Tup-perware container when she doesn't ac-tually own any Tupperware, and what she REALLY means is for them to use one of the twenty-seven recycled butter tubs (with missing lids) that comprise the bulk of her food-storage system.

A real superwoman would never in-vite friends over for homemade brownies, forget to add the flour, and make her guests eat the brownies using spoons. She definitely would not then move to a new house, invite those same friends over for chili, realize her spoons were still packed away in the garage somewhere, and serve the chili with plastic forks.

A real superwoman would never hang up on her editor while shouting the phrase, "I HAVE TO GO! THE BABY'S IN THE TOILET!"

A real superwoman would not own a freezer so precari-ously crammed with frozen mystery foods that she makes her children wear hard hats and steel-toed boots before they're allowed to open the door for ice cubes.

A real superwoman would never admit to a friend that her definition of a home-cooked meal means any meal requir-ing more than two boxes or cans.

A real superwoman would not occasionally arrive at her office at 6:00 A.M. to get some extra work done and fall asleep at her computer until 8:00. Thus, she would never be put in the embarrassing position of hoping desperately that her coworkers wouldn't find out about her dark secret, only to have one of them tell her later, "Of course we knew. We all knew. When you'd been sleeping, you'd come out of your office with a keyboard imprint on your cheek."

A real superwoman would not be growing eleven different strains of penicillin in her refrigerator.

A real superwoman would never sit down in front of the TV to watch *Sesame Street* with her toddler . . . and still be sitting there watching Barney two hours later while her toddler is happily playing with her blocks in the other room.

A real superwoman has never stood in front of her closet, gazed at the pile of dirty laundry awaiting her, and had the word "Kilimanjaro" pop, unbidden, into her mind.

## You Might Be a Superwoman If . . .

I guess we've pretty well established that I'm not Superwoman. Despite my occasional delusions of grandeur, I don't have to spend too much time reflecting about my life to bring myself back to reality.

But what about you? Maybe you've never had experiences like mine. It's possible that you've never served brownies with a spoon or chili with a fork, nor shaved your chin, nor spotted a mountain goat disappearing around the crest of your laundry.

Who knows? Maybe you're the real thing. Maybe your life is "together" in a way that the rest of us only get to dream about. Just in case, I've compiled a brief list of characteristics of a real superwoman. If you'd like, circle the statements that apply to you and let's see how close you can come.

If there is a fresh box of baking soda in your refrigerator . . .

If your husband goes to work each and every morning with a smile on his face . . .

If your children love green vegetables and watch less than one hour of TV each day . . .

> you might be a real superwoman.

If you've never taken store-bought food to a potluck . . .

If you always remember to floss and have the energy to complete a skin-care regimen every night . . .

If your scrapbooks are up-to-date and your children's baby books have anecdotes and pictures after they were two months old . . .

> you might be a real superwoman.

If you wish you could enjoy reading Erma Bombeck but you just can't relate to any of her confessions . . .

If you've never paid good money for an exercise tape that, even as we speak, is still in cellophane on a shelf somewhere in your home . . .

If you've never felt a surge of panic at 7:30 A.M. when your husband calls innocently from the closet: "Honey? Where are the clean shirts?" . . .

> you might actually be a real superwoman.

If you've never obsessed about overdressing for a party . . .

If you think shopping for a new bathing suit sounds like a fun way to spend an afternoon . . .

If you've never laughed a little too hard and hoped desperately that the ensuing embarrassing noise wasn't yours . . .

> it's possible that you just might be a real superwoman.

179

If you've had the same checking account for years and have never had to close it to figure out what your balance was . . .

If you used to own a set of "Days of the Week" panties and never wore the wrong panty on the wrong day . . .

If you wouldn't think twice about buying a house with a clear-glass shower door . . .

there's a good chance that you're a real superwoman.

## Super Women of the World, Unite!

So how did you do? If you circled more than half of the statements, please write to me (my E-mail address and P.O. box number are at the end of this book). I'd like to get your autograph and maybe even alert Oprah and 20/20.

*Women of steel? Women who leap tall buildings? They're the women who drive carpools and care for aging parents, who watch Barney, watch for their teens to come home after curfew, and watch their weight.*

If you didn't do so hot, cheer up and welcome to the club. You and I are members of a mega-sorority of women everywhere who live a harried, flawed—and at the same time, a relatively happy—existence.

Superwoman? Who needs her? She doesn't exist, my friend. Not at my house, not at yours. Not in our generation. Not in this universe.

Superwoman is passé.

But *super women* . . . well, that's another story altogether.

Let me tell you a little bit about super women. They're everywhere, in every generation, in big cities and small burgs alike. They're flawed and fabulous, wounded and wonderful. They are moms and wives and daughters just like you and me, women who know what it's like to juggle and struggle, live and learn, laugh and love, moan and groan, and ultimately survive and even thrive.

Women of steel? Women who leap tall buildings? They're the women who drive carpools and care for aging parents, who watch Barney, watch for their teens to come home after curfew, and watch their weight. They're the women who remember birthdays and doctor's appointments and baseball games, who bake cookies for fund-raisers and muffins for colleagues at the office. They're the women who take care of grandkids so their daughters can work. They crave chocolate and hate well-woman exams and learn to live with the adversities of life. They're the women who change diapers and dread the change of life and end up changing their world because of what they do and who they are.

Super women? They're alive and well on Planet Earth.

So smile when you zip up that cape.

Looks like we just might be the real thing, after all.

### Challenge Those Unrealistic Expectations!

Are we trying to have it all, do it all, be it all? Maybe it's time to abandon unrealistic expectations and give ourselves a break.

*Do we feel guilty that our kitchen floors are not clean enough to eat from?* Who eats off the kitchen floor anyway! Well, okay, babies do. But they also put things in their mouths from the carpet, the driveway, and the doggie dish, so they don't count. If I don't have time to mop the kitchen

181

floor, I spot-clean. I take a wet dishcloth, drop it on the floor, step on it, and slip and slide over dirty spots. My floor is presentable within minutes.

*Do we obsess over the fact that we don't have time to bake seventeen varieties of holiday cookies?* Spend two hours making six dozen of ONE cookie (you'll be amazed how quickly you can do this). Then call five friends and have them do the same thing. One Saturday afternoon, host a cookie exchange: every participant will end up with a dozen of six different holiday cookies. Once these have been eaten, buy Oreos. Statistics say that the average American gains nine pounds between Thanksgiving and New Year's. While there's nothing wrong with having holiday treats around the house, we don't really need an unlimited supply. So relax. Nobody needs to be greasing cookie sheets at 2:00 A.M. And we don't need to feel guilty about it either.

*Are we guilt-ridden that we aren't spending enough quality time with our families?* This one's easy. Take the time you save by NOT mopping the kitchen floor and NOT outbaking those Keebler elves and go play Monopoly with your kids or seduce your husband. Projects can be put on hold or even abandoned. People can't.

## Myth #15

# Better Safe Than Sorry

 e were waiting for a flight out of DFW airport, en route to California for Thanksgiving, when it dawned on me that I needed to go to the bathroom. To avoid having to take care of business in a space roughly the size of a phone booth, I decided to visit the ladies' room before boarding the plane. I told Larry I would be back in a moment and held out one end of a fluorescent-yellow dog leash.

He recoiled. "I don't have to actually hold it, do I?"

"Of course you do. I'll just be a moment."

"Karen, people stare."

"How hard can this be? Just hang on." I tried to put it in his hand. "You have to close your fingers, though."

"This is embarrassing."

We both looked down at Kacie where she sat on the floor, untying Larry's shoelaces. Within the space of about a heartbeat she wobbled to her feet, smiled up at us, and bolted for the nearest exit. She got three feet away before the leash pulled taut and she landed hard on a well-padded bottom.

"See? This leash is a lifesaver. Now stop complaining and let me go to the bathroom."

"Karen, it's not even a baby harness. It's *really* a dog leash. How could you?"

"Misty Penny won't even miss it. I couldn't find the baby harness; I think Kaitlyn used it for a science project. Now if you don't mind, I've really got to go . . ."

"People even make comments. Don't you care when they make comments? When we were at the security station I heard a woman say, 'Look at that poor baby.' Doesn't that bother you?"

I sighed. "That woman is not responsible for keeping an eighteen-month-old safe in a crowded airport. I am. I couldn't care less what she thinks. I'm far more concerned what people will say when they see a grown woman straddling a yellow puddle on the floor. Can I go now?"

*We hold on tight, harboring our growing babies from injuries both physical and emotional. And yet our ultimate goal as parents is not to hold them close, but to set them free, pushing them from our sheltered nests and watching them fly.*

My story has a happy ending. I eventually made it to the bathroom, and Kacie made it to California.

Keeping children safe is such a challenge! And it only gets tougher as they grow: The dog leash that works wonders with a two-year-old doesn't help much with a child who is fifteen (although I know some parents who would be willing to give it a try).

184

Whether we are the parents of toddlers or teens, adolescents or adults, we care about the well-being of our children. In fact, we go to great measures to protect them from all of the unpleasantries that the world has to offer.

We buy leashes and child gates, outlet plugs and Ipecac. We help them memorize our phone number and teach them about 911. We buy bicycle helmets and insist that they wear knee pads when they skate. We make them walk, not run, when by a pool. We keep them from playing with sharp objects, and we remind them (daily) to stop leaning backward in chairs before they fall and break their necks.

We warn them about sex and alcohol and drugs. We eyeball their friends, enforce curfews, establish rules. We try to shield them from questionable movies, and we always make them tell us where they're going whenever they leave home.

Sometimes, we even try to protect them from themselves.

We hold on tight, harboring our growing babies from strangers and germs, accidents and disappointments, injuries both physical and emotional. And yet our ultimate goal as parents is not to hold them close, but to set them free, pushing them from our sheltered nests and watching them fly.

Of course, herein lies the beauty and the pain of parenting. There is, indeed, an exquisite tension between hanging on and letting go, between dependence and independence, between knowing when to keep them safe and knowing when to let them risk.

Can we hang on too tight? Is safety our ultimate goal, or is it growth? Can we consistently provide both, or does the time come when we have to choose between the two?

## Overprotective Parents of the World, Unite!

When I was growing up, I was convinced that my parents were too protective. Looking back, I might even have been right! After all, how else can you explain the fact that my dad

185

didn't trust anyone's driving but his own? (For several years, even grandparents were not on the "approved driver" list.) Or the fact that my parents turned down my desperate pleas to take trumpet lessons, explaining: "If you take trumpet lessons, you'll want to play in the high school band. And if you play in the high school band, you'll have to travel to games. And if you travel to games, you'll want to ride in the school bus with all your friends, and we don't know anything at all about the bus driver. So, no, you can't take trumpet lessons."

But I shouldn't complain. Several decades later, I have to admit that their rules, regulations, and curfews got me to adulthood fairly intact, and now that I'm a parent myself, I wouldn't change a thing about the years I spent in my childhood home.

For example, I wouldn't change the fact that I wasn't allowed to go on dates until my sixteenth birthday. Naturally, I hated this rule when I was fourteen, but as the parent of two daughters, this rule is looking better to me all the time.

I wouldn't change the fact that my dates weren't allowed to drive on the freeway with me in the car. Of course, this was often inconvenient: I frequently had to explain to boyfriends how to get from my house to Disneyland via side streets. But now I realize that the experience built character. It also established some unspoken boundaries: Once a date realized he couldn't get above forty mph with me in the front seat, getting anywhere at all in the backseat seemed pretty much out of the question.

I wouldn't even change the fact that I wasn't allowed to see movies at the drive-in. I fudged on this one, though. When I was eighteen, I went on a date while my parents were out of town and discovered for myself why drive-ins are not a good environment for hormonally driven teenagers. Years later, I went to a drive-in again, this time with my husband of two years. If I remember correctly, it wasn't nearly as much fun: Larry actually wanted to watch the movie.

I guess when you become a parent yourself, some things come full circle. Some people would say that, when it comes to raising my two kids, I'm overprotective, too.

I experienced a breakthrough this past summer, though. My daughter, then nine, spent a week at church camp half an hour from our home. Several hours after dropping her off at camp, I came to the conclusion that she might not be warm enough, and returned to camp bearing gifts of blankets. The next day I showed up with extra sunscreen. By the third day, my husband and a friend, Jerry Spurlock, were ribbing me so much that I decided maybe I should stay home. By the fourth day, I was furious at myself for letting Kaitlyn attend camp, and I was quite convinced that church camp is a barbaric and unnecessary ritual that should be purged from any civilized society.

*Once a date realized he couldn't get above forty mph with me in the front seat, getting anywhere at all in the backseat seemed pretty much out of the question.*

On the fifth and last day of camp, I drove to Camp Lebannon. Filled with anticipation and relief, I parked my car and walked across a blanket of pine needles to meet Kaitlyn at her cabin. I watched as other parents experienced Hallmark reunions with their children, yet Kaitlyn was nowhere in sight. I waited, anxious, until I spotted my daughter approaching with a friend, engrossed in animated conversation. My eyes glistened to see her. Had she missed me as much as I'd missed her? Would she cry with happiness? Would I?

"Hi, Mom." She waved as she passed by.

Had it only been five days? She was taller. She was tanner. Her hair was tangled and there were scabs on both knees. But the biggest change was an independent confidence that hadn't been there when I'd seen her last.

187

Driving home in the car, she jabbered enthusiastically about her week. She mentioned water balloon battles and shaving cream wars, cafeteria mystery foods and new friends and more. But the thing she mentioned most often was chapel.

She talked about missionaries she had met and worship songs she had learned and speakers who had challenged her young faith. She used the word "awesome" at least a dozen times. And then she made me promise to let her return to camp next summer.

I agreed in a heartbeat.

Maybe I was wrong about camp being barbaric and unnecessary. After all, it proved to be a stretching experience, one that resulted in new maturity and growth. Yes, there was separation and even risk, but after it was all over, the benefits seemed more than apparent.

Besides, it was good for Kaitlyn, too.

## Disappointment Smarts—And Can Make Us Wiser

Whenever we allow our kids to venture beyond our front doors to experience some new challenge, we are taking a calculated risk. Sometimes nothing bad happens: Our kids experience success, growth, *and* safety, and we breathe a sigh of relief.

Sometimes there are physical injuries such as skinned knees, end-zone bruises, rollerblade burns, and more. We break open the first-aid kit or call our pediatrician, all the while shaking our heads and wishing we could spare our kids the "owies" that seem to accompany a life lived with enthusiasm.

There are times, however, when success seems elusive, and the resulting scrapes and scars aren't the kind that can be mended with a Band-Aid or even a cast.

Painful memories from my youth include the time I abused certain privileges and dated a young man behind my parents' back . . . until they found out! I was fifteen and in love, and the pain of losing this relationship was exceeded only by the pain I felt when I realized how much I had betrayed my parents by my choices.

They include the rejection I felt when I entered a teen beauty pageant and didn't win. Didn't even place.

They include the disillusionment I experienced when one young man I dated turned out to be a pathological liar (even his appearance was a lie: My prince with the jet black hair was actually a towhead. Go figure!).

And yet . . .

Would it have been better for my parents never to have gifted me with their trust in the first place? Should embarrassment and fear have kept me from entering the pageant? Would it have been better to never have dated rather than put my heart on the line in dating relationships that failed?

*Love and trust, confidence and courage, integrity and self-respect . . . these concepts have come to mean more from the valleys I've travailed than from the mountaintops I've scaled.*

In her article "Moving On," Diane Burton Robb tells the story of disappointments in her life, and how it's possible to transform "the stuff of broken dreams into the substance of living." She writes: "To believe that all bad things can be changed into good is a philosophy destined to disillusion. But the debris of loss has its usefulness. It rebuilds hope. Sometimes, sparkling among the ruins, treasures can be found: courage, resolve and finally self-acceptance" (*Guideposts,* December 1992).

I know that I've been shaped, honed, and grown by the disappointments in my life. Love and trust, confidence and courage, integrity and self-respect . . . these concepts and others have come to mean more from the valleys I've travailed than from the mountaintops I've scaled.

What about our kids?

On one hand, I would love to protect Kaitlyn and Kacie from their own mistakes, from rejection, from disillusionment, from all the disappointments and hard knocks that are part and parcel of life.

On the other hand . . .

**Moms are bred to rescue. We're like Saint Bernards, but with better breath.**

I know that's not possible. I know I can't protect them from the world. Besides, even if I could . . . if it were somehow within my power . . . if I were smart enough, strong enough, wise enough . . . would I do it even then?

If I were that smart and strong and wise, I'd be like God. And if I were like God, I'd probably do well to do what he does, which is walk beside his kids each step of the way, letting them live and learn, loving them completely, and helping them pick up the pieces when their world shatters around them.

## Natural Consequences Make Good Sense

We can't protect our kids from everything. And even if we could, we wouldn't . . . or at least we *shouldn't*. Yet there's got to be a balance. Isn't there some way we can safeguard them from some of life's greater tragedies while still giving them the space they need to live and learn?

Sometimes, when we're raising our kids, the best way to keep them from succumbing to great harm later is to allow them to experience some small harm today. I remember trying to teach my first baby the concept of "hot." Kaitlyn would get near the stove and I would say, "Hot." She would approach the running tub before I could adjust the water and I would say "Hot." Each time this happened, she looked at me with a blank smile. She was probably thinking, "My mom's a moron. She just said the large white appliance beneath that boiling pot of spaghetti is named 'hot.' Now she's telling me this transparent steaming liquid also goes by the name of 'hot.' Maybe I should get someone else to help me with my vocabulary."

One day it dawned on me she would never know what I was talking about until I allowed her to touch something hot. I chose carefully. It had to be something that would provide discomfort without injury. I selected a piece of toast still hot enough to melt a pat of butter. I told Kaitlyn it was hot, warned her not to touch it, and then didn't stop her when she did.

She jerked her hand away and said, "Oh. Hot."

That was nine years ago, and I'm still looking for ways I can put natural consequences to work for my kids, inflicting discomfort today so that real damage and even tragedy might be averted tomorrow.

Of course, you and I both know that this is easier said than done. Parents—and particularly mothers—are bred to rescue. We're like Saint Bernards, but with better breath. Did my fourth grader put off completing her book report until eight o'clock Sunday night despite the fact that I reminded her almost hourly throughout the weekend? I'm tempted to write half of the report for her so she can at least get to bed by ten, when what I really should do is tell her to set her alarm an hour early, do what she can before school, and let consequences fall where they may.

Did my seventh grader neglect to mow the lawn, despite the fact that he needed the accompanying ten-dollar payment to go with his friends to the movies? My tendency would be to advance the money, when what I probably should do is remind him that the LAST time I advanced him money the lawn never got mowed at all, then break the news that this time the bank is closed. Too bad, so sad.

A friend of mine doesn't beg his children to clean their rooms. Ed believes that responsible stewardship is the price that goes with the privilege of having a bedroom. If the responsibility isn't met, the most natural consequence he can think of is for the privilege to be revoked. This is why, when his children don't heed a gentle reminder to clean their rooms, they get evicted. They sleep with blankets and pillows in the hallway, and lose access to their rooms for any activity that doesn't result in being able to see the floor again.

*We can tie them to us when they're small. We can give them some freedoms as they grow. But the day always comes when apron strings have served their purpose and must be done away with for good.*

Two years ago, Kaitlyn and I locked horns over something silly. It was eight o'clock on a school night and I asked her to finish her bath so she could get to bed at a decent hour. She dallied. I directed. She disagreed. I demanded. She defied.

At that point I was ready to go into orbit. Her last words to me had been along the lines of ". . . and you can't make me," and I wondered if she was right.

That's when I took a risk and tried something new. I let her experience the natural consequences of her choice to disobey.

I explained to her: "Kaitlyn, you want the power to decide when to disobey, how long to stay in the bath, and how long to stay up. Alright, for one night I'm going to let you have that power and see what you do with it. From this moment, you're on your own. Stay in the tub as long as you want. Stay up as long as you want. But if you're old enough to make a decision to disobey and take rebellious control of your life, you're certainly old enough to get yourself ready for bed. You know where your pajamas are. You know where your toothbrush is. You know where your bedroom is. When you're in bed, I'll come in and say good-night. Until then, you're on your own."

192

Kaitlyn was livid, which I thought she might be: She truly hated preparing for bed by herself. I left the bathroom to the sound of her screaming for me to help her get ready for bed. She sat in cold water for nearly an hour demanding/yelling/begging/ordering me to help her. It was after ten o'clock before she finally dragged herself out of the tub and into her pajamas, her voice hoarse, eyes swollen, and skin wrinkled nearly past recognition.

The next day I was driving carpool when I overheard Kaitlyn describing the experience to her friends: "I was so tired this morning I couldn't hardly get out of bed! Last night I fought my mom for control, and so she let me have the control to get myself out of the tub and into bed completely on my own. It was awful! I'll never do THAT again, let me tell you!"

Sometimes kids need to be rescued. You and I both know this. There are times, however, when the best approach is to let nature take its course. There are tough lessons to be learned in this manner, lessons about consequences and ramifications and cause-and-effect. But our kids will hurt less learning these lessons now, when they are young, when the stakes are not as high as they will be in just a few short years!

## Apron Strings Are Meant to Be Snipped

We can tie them to us when they're small. We can give them some freedoms as they grow. But the day always comes when apron strings have served their purpose and must be done away with for good.

My friend Cherie told me that when her son, Daniel, turned eighteen, she bought him an unusual gift. She drove to the mall, found a store specializing in cookery and kitchen accessories, and bought him an apron.

It wasn't even a manly chef's apron. It was frilly and delicate and petite.

I imagine that when Daniel opened the box, his first thought was that the clerk had mixed up the nametags; that there was a mother somewhere who was, at that very moment, opening the car stereo speakers that belonged to him.

But his parents just nodded for him to continue.

He lifted the apron from the box, and found a pair of scissors. And then he began to grin.

In ceremonious fashion, Cherie and Jerry held the apron while Daniel took the scissors and with a snip, cut the apron strings.

Two years later, he says of the experience, "It was cool. I liked it. It put into words things that had never been said, things like, 'We've brought you up, we've done our job, and now you're in charge. We'll still be here for you, but you've got to make your own decisions now.' It was a big responsibility. Sobering. Reality. I knew it was time to grow up."

Growing up. Cutting strings. Giving freedoms. Letting go.

Our children begin their lives in our wombs, bound to us by a cord. By the time they are young adults, they are independent in so many ways! It would be nice if that independence came easily, without risks and mistakes and danger and even the pain of harsh lessons learned. But ask any veteran of war: Independence always comes with a price!

Parenting. What an odd assignment of love we have been given; what a dichotomous assortment of duties we are asked to perform! We hang on and let go . . . encourage dependence while we prepare for independence . . . keep them safe and let them risk.

Our strategies change. But our motivation never does.

It's called love.

## Myth #16

# A Dog Is a Man's Best Friend

Families and pets just seem to go together. Kind of like cake and candles. Or Christmas and mistletoe. Or bacon and eggs.

Which reminds me of the time I had a bunch of baby chickens as pets. I was about eight and figured I could avoid the time-consuming task of giving my pets fresh water every day if I replaced their shallow drinking saucer with a bucket filled with enough $H_2O$ to last, say, a week.

You can probably guess what happened. Let it suffice to say that I had no idea baby chickens had such poor balance.

The good news is that we saved every last one, fishing them out of the bucket and nursing them back to health with hair dryers, heating pads, and even lightbulbs. Within a few hours, all my pets were happy and dry, which is more than I can say for myself. If memory serves me correctly, I was in hot water for a long time over that one.

Families and pets. What a combination. The potential for disaster seems infinite. On the other hand, perhaps it's not a bad idea to let small children practice a few years with pets before we ever let them in the same room with an actual sibling.

## Animal Mayhem

I shouldn't be too hard on myself about the baby-chicken fiasco. It's not surprising. In fact, when you consider my family background, the thing that's truly surprising is that any of us are allowed to have pets at all. If animals could blacklist certain families from pet ownership, we'd never be allowed within ten feet of a Habitrail.

I think it all started with my grandfather. Growing up on a dairy farm, one of his daily chores was milking the cows. The downside of this chore was that he frequently got lashed across the face by the tail of whatever cow was being milked. That's when he devised a new system: He tied the tails of the cows together, milked them in peace, and then untied the cows and turned them out to pasture. The system worked great . . . until the day he forgot one critical step. My grandfather had finished milking and was occupied with some new task when he heard an unearthly bellowing coming from the pasture. Remembering that he had forgotten to untie the tails, he raced toward the sound. When he arrived at the pasture gate he discovered that one cow had two tails and another cow had none.

During this same period of time my grandmother was growing up across town. She tells a story of the time she and her brother Ed were playing in the kitchen with a pet duck when they got curious about something. They wondered what would happen if they fed the duck some black pepper. The

196

good news is that the duck survived the experiment. The bad news is that his bill turned red and he got very, very thirsty.

It shouldn't come as any surprise that this couple married and had children who had weird experiences with pets. Years after the duck incident my grandmother observed her two-year-old son admiring several goldfish swimming in a bowl. Several minutes later she walked back past the fishbowl. Richard was gone, and one of the fish had a bite taken out of it.

## Revenge à la Rover

A lot of pet stories can fit into two categories: Things We Do to Them and Things They Do to Us. The fact that pets can create dilemmas and embarrassing moments for their owners should help absolve some of the guilt we feel over the fact that we are less than perfect masters. I mean, it's not like animals are complete victims. They're capable of exacting revenge now and then for the mistakes that we make.

Take, for example, our golden retriever, Misty Penny. One spring morning when she was six months old I was awakened at six in the morning by barking. I padded downstairs and into the backyard to make sure she had food and water. She had plenty of both, so I came back to bed. At a new round of barking, I found myself standing on the back porch in my nightgown, inspecting Misty's muddy paws for burrs. Nothing. On my third excursion downstairs, I was running my hands through Misty's fur looking for *anything* that might be causing her to jeopardize her happy home by driving me to distraction with her yapping, when I noticed something. I couldn't believe I'd been so stupid! No wonder Misty was barking ferociously: She knew time was running out. In a few more days she would have been lucky to squeak like a chew toy.

This was due to the circumference of Misty's collar. You see, I had buckled a collar on her when we brought her home at six weeks, and then . . . well, the thought had never really crossed my mind to, you know . . .

. . . I hate to even admit it . . .

. . . enlarge the collar.

WIPE THAT DISGUSTED LOOK OFF YOUR FACE!

I wasn't trying to be cruel to an animal. I just forgot. Anyway, the collar fit about as comfortably as an overzealous blood pressure cuff. Luckily, as soon as I loosened it Misty stopped barking and gave me that puppy-dog look that let me know she'd forgiven me.

Or so I thought.

My guess is that Misty was thinking about that collar each of the two dozen times she used my living room carpet as a toilet. She was thinking about that collar three or four times daily as she sloppily licked the fresh Windex off the glass panes of my French doors. And she was definitely thinking about the collar as she dug her way through the wood planks on the back porch.

*Fish, hamsters, lizards, cats, rabbits, puppies, birds, and more . . . somehow we just can't resist the urge to enliven our lives with a little help from the Wild Kingdom.*

Of course I'm joking. Dogs aren't revengeful creatures. They would never try to ruin our lives on purpose.

Most of the time it happens quite by accident.

Take Bernie for example. Bernie is a collie mix who lives with a friend of ours named Sherry. Sherry was away from home when Bernie figured out how to shimmy open the back door—from the outside. This, of course, triggered the burglar alarm. In fact, Bernie managed to trigger the alarm five times that afternoon, drawing the police to the home on two separate occasions. By the time the officials figured it all out, they were dog-tired of the whole thing. When Sherry got home, she discovered that the city had a bone to pick with her: It seems she had broken some ordinance or another and ended up being slapped with a fine. As you can imagine, Bernie was *really* in the doghouse after that.

We've all got pet stories, and no wonder! Trying to meld the lives of a houseful of human beings is hard enough. Trying to merge people with other people while adding in an animal or two is a little like trying to bake a cake while blindfolded: The results may not be what you expected, but at least they're good for a laugh.

And yet we keep doing it, don't we? Fish, hamsters, lizards, cats, rabbits, puppies, birds, and more . . . somehow we just can't resist the urge to enliven our lives with a little help from the Wild Kingdom.

Why is that?

One reason might be that, in the balance of things, most of us figure that pets are worth the trouble. The benefits we receive from our fine furry friends must, in some economy of life, outweigh the trouble and expense.

Either that or we're slow learners.


## Choosing the Right Pet

What makes pet ownership a successful, happy experience? Helen Cariotis is an animal trainer and the owner of Canine Counselors of Duncanville, Texas. She teaches obedience classes, speaks on pet safety at local schools, and can even be hired for private counseling where she visits homes and helps animal lovers deal with annoying behavior problems exhibited by Fido or Mittens.

According to Helen, success may well be determined by the amount of research that goes into choosing the right pet. "In my experience," she says, "the average person will spend more time researching a washer and dryer than the dog that will be a part of their family for years to come. You'd be surprised how much of my business comes from people who go out and get a Siberian Husky—despite the fact that they live in an apartment!"

When families approach her for help in choosing the right pet, Helen begins by having family members complete a test to determine what they are looking for in a pet. She tries to match lifestyle choices with known traits exhibited by various breeds. She explains:

"A lot of people like labs. And no wonder: They are wonderful dogs—great with kids. You'd have to set one on fire to get it to bite you. But when they're young, they're live wires. Energetic, bouncy, and a lot of people aren't ready for that. They've seen sedate older dogs leading blind people. They're not prepared for puppyhood and having to peel their dog off the wall.

"Or people will get a collie, sheltie, or German shepherd and then complain that the dogs spend the whole day chasing kids and nipping heels. Well, of course they do. They're herding dogs.

"Jack Russell terriers are very popular right now. That's the kind of dog you see on TV when you watch the show *Wishbone*. Terriers are great dogs, active, healthy . . . but they're bred to dig and to hunt little furry things. They're tenacious. If your dog wants to get through a closed door at your house, he just may sit down and dig his way through. People see Wishbone on TV and think 'That's the dog for me,' not realizing that it took more than $30,000 in training to get Wishbone where he is today! People need to spend a little time learning about the animal they are considering rather than running out and making an impulsive decision."

To help your family choose a pet that will be compatible with your unique needs, Helen makes the following suggestions:

- Check out the book *The Right Dog for You* by Daniel Tortora. The book examines traits of various breeds and includes a test you can take to identify the kind of pet that will fit well with your lifestyle.

- Talk to your local veterinarian.
- Call breeders and trainers and ask their opinions about specific breeds.
- Talk to friends and neighbors about their experiences with various pets.
- Visit dog shows and ask pet owners about the personality traits and temperaments of different breeds.

## First-Pet Protocol

Of course, there are other things to ponder besides breed of animal, particularly if you are considering a first pet, or have small children in your home. Here are some strategies for families looking to embark on an animal adventure for the very first time.

*If you have small children, you may want to consider a large dog rather than a small one.* Most bites occur when dogs are startled or threatened. Small dogs are often more hyper and startle more easily than large dogs. They also are more vulnerable to the poking and prodding, jumping and bouncing of small children. Large dogs, in contrast, will not feel as threatened due to their size and may tolerate the playfulness of children better than small dogs.

*For a first pet, you may want to consider a cat.* Their feline independence makes them a good choice while children are learning the ropes of responsibility. If kids forget to take the puppy outside for a potty break, a crisis can occur; if they forget to empty the litter box, life goes on relatively undisturbed. If you leave your home on vacation, a dog will require care while you are gone. A cat, on the other hand, can be left home alone for several days with adequate food and water.

*Don't saddle small children with the bulk of responsibility for a new pet.* No matter how much you nag, a six-year-old is not prepared to successfully assume the daily care of an animal. Until a child can handle his or her own daily responsibilities (brushing teeth, making bed, doing homework) without incessant nagging from a parent, he's probably not ready for his own pet.

> *"People tend to buy pets so kids can learn responsibility. More than responsibility, pets teach children about compassion."*

Another reason not to give a child sole responsibility for an animal such as a puppy is that dogs tend to view small children as peers. Helen says: "Dogs want to know who's in charge. Very few dogs are going to look at small kids as having any authority. While they will obey a command from an adult, dogs will often ignore commands given by a child. Don't set your younger child up for failure by giving him more responsibility than he can handle." Helen suggests making pets a family affair, with the parents assuming ultimate responsibility until children are in junior high or older.

"People tend to buy pets so kids can learn responsibility," she says. "I think, more than responsibility, pets teach children about compassion. In caring for an animal, a child learns that other living things have needs. They need to be loved. They need to be fed. Sometimes they even need to be left alone. Animals teach kids, 'Respect my space. Leave me alone when I'm sleeping. Don't poke or bully or pull my ears or I might growl or nip. Play with me, but play gentle. Snuggling is good. I get hungry, too.' Responsibility is good. But compassion and empathy may be even better."

### Quality Time Isn't Just for Children!

People are drawn to a wide variety of animals as pets. But one of the most popular, by far, is puppies.

I asked Helen to name some common "pet pitfalls" that new owners often experience. When training a new puppy and trying to incorporate him into a family, what are some widespread mistakes or misconceptions, and how can we avoid them?

According to Helen, the single biggest mistake that new owners make is failing to bond with their new puppy. The first twenty weeks are the most important. During this time, the forging of a strong people/puppy bond goes a long way to establish the love and loyalty that will make your job as dog owner a lot simpler.

Helen says: "Dogs are the only animals that will do things for us by choice. Give a horse the choice of pulling a plow or going back to the barn and he's outta' there. But dogs crave socialization and will do anything for people with whom they bond. People don't understand this. They send their dogs away to be trained, and then don't understand why the dog will perform for the trainer and not for them. It's all about relationship. Invest the time it takes to bond with your puppy in the first four to five months and it will make a lifelong difference in that dog."

*Pets also teach us about joy. Dogs, for example, are perennial two-year-olds. They love to play and take things at face value, living life with an exuberant joy that we might be wise to emulate.*

Bonding is so critical, Helen says, that she suggests an adult make arrangements to be home with a new puppy for a week or so. This time is critical for bonding, but also for behavior reinforcement. "If you bring a puppy home and then go to work from seven to six each day, you're leaving him to grow up on his own, making decisions that are in the best interest of a dog and not in the best interest of your family. If he does something appropriate, such as barking when a stranger comes to the door, there's no one around to tell him he did a good job. If he does something inappropriate, such as napping on the sofa, there's no one to tell him that's not good."

She suggests: "If you work outside your home, arrange for some vacation time to be home. If that's not possible, try to come home during your lunch hour, or pay a little extra and get a pet sitter who can at least provide appropriate re-inforcement for a week or two until your puppy begins to learn your rules. It may seem extreme, but in the long run you'll be happy you did it."

## The Joys of Pet Ownership

Pets add a lot to our lives. What are some of the things we get from our pets? I mean, besides fleas.

We've talked about the fact that pets teach children about responsibility and, perhaps of greater importance, compassion.

Pets also teach us about joy. Dogs, for example, are peren-nial two-year-olds. They love to play and take things at face value, living life with an exuberant joy that we might be wise to emulate.

Pets also provide companionship. The people/animal bond can be powerful, not to mention the connection that they can spark with other humans. Walking the dog gets us out of the house and often into the path of other pet enthu-siasts. And animals are icebreakers; they give us something to talk about with other people who also know the value of a good canine companion or feline friend.

They can even make us healthier. Research has proven that people who own pets often live longer than those who don't!

Finally, pets can provide a sense of security, barking at noises and things that go bump in the night. Besides, com-pany is always comforting, even if the company does have a wet nose and likes to chew on old shoes.

Are dogs man's best friend? I don't know that I would go that far, but I think it's safe to say that they are friends. And in a fast-paced and sometimes hostile world, I guess you can never have too many friends.

Even if they do answer to "Spot."

## Keeping Pets from Becoming Pet Peeves

Choosing a pet for your family? Careful research can mean the difference between a successful experience and a fiasco. Animal trainer Helen Cariotis suggests the following:

- Looking for a dog? Check out the book *The Right Dog for You* by Daniel Tortora. The book examines traits of various breeds and includes a test you can take to identify the kind of pet that will fit well with your lifestyle.
- Talk to your local veterinarian.
- Call breeders and trainers and ask their opinion about specific breeds.
- Talk to friends and neighbors about their experience with various pets.
- Visit dog shows and ask pet owners about the personality traits and temperaments of different breeds.

## Myth #17

# And They Lived Happily Ever After

I believe that every story has a happy ending.

Of course, I also believe in Santa Claus and the Tooth Fairy and that Bill Clinton never inhaled.

Unfortunately, unhappy endings are part and parcel of family life. Whether they come in the form of the fifteen-year-old who doesn't get invited to the school dance, or the father who gets laid off two weeks before Christmas, or divorce or disability or death, disappointment and sadness are unavoidable companions on the journey of life.

I didn't always understand this profound principle of life. As part of the Cinderella Generation, I was weaned on fairy tales and thought the Cleavers were distant cousins. If life was a road, I figured it was a shining highway, with few bumps or detours along the way.

Now I know that life is not as much a highway as it is an unblazed frontier, and that negotiating the terrain means leaving the convertible at home and bringing along a four-wheel drive and a good compass.

*There's something about a two-pound bag of M&M's that can salve nearly any wound the world inflicts.*

Life is a bumpy ride, folks.

Despite our best intentions and most ardent desires, everyone doesn't live happily ever after. The boy doesn't always get the girl (and even if he does, divorce statistics say he may not keep her). The nice guy, indeed, finishes last more often than we like to admit. And, yes, bad things really do happen to good people.

When an unhappy ending comes our way, the good news is that we have a choice regarding how we're going to respond. In fact, you and I have a wide spectrum of helpful resources, stress-busting techniques, and coping mechanisms from which to choose.

What kind of resources?

Eating chocolate, of course, tops the chart for most women. And for good reason: There's something about a two-pound bag of M&M's that can salve nearly any wound the world inflicts. (Non-chocolate sugary foods work too. Once, driven by PMS and work deadlines, I called bosom-buddy Linda Holland and cried, "Help! I've just eaten half a box of Cap'n Crunch cereal!" I knew she was a kindred spirit who had "been there, done that" when she immediately responded, "Ouch! Do you know what that'll do to the roof of your mouth?")

Which brings to mind another survival tool: Friendships are, of course, a must-have resource in times of trouble. Despite the fact that when we are hurting we are often tempted to withdraw into ourselves, the ability to reach out—and allow others to reach in—can provide a safe harbor in stormy seas.

*I wouldn't even be surprised to learn that someone has discovered the fountain of youth, but lobbyists for greeting card companies are putting pressure on legislators to keep this information under wraps.*

Indulging in comfort food . . . confiding in a good friend . . . as well as jogging around the block . . . having a good cry . . . telling your woeful tale to a pastor or counselor . . . recording your fears and feelings in a journal . . . turning your problems into prayers . . . letting your personal pain propel you into helping others in similar straits . . . these are just a few of the choices we can make when we come face-to-face with one of the many chapters in our lives in which a happy ending seems well beyond our grasp.

## Draw Your Bow with Curly, Larry, and Moe

When life plays a little too rough and you feel the need to defend your sanity, there is yet another option in your arsenal: Take aim with humor. A good belly-laugh is potent—it can soften the blow of many of life's disappointments.

Seldom is humor more aptly applied than when it is wielded on the topic of aging. Aging qualifies, after all, as one of life's more poignant little disappointments. In fact, I'm of the opinion that having to cope with the gradual decline of our bodies is nothing less than a bummer of a way to have to live out the final chapters of our lives.

But humor helps us cope, doesn't it?

In fact, laughing at advancing age has become a multi-million dollar industry. I wouldn't even be surprised to learn that someone has discovered the fountain of youth, but lobbyists for greeting card companies are putting pressure on legislators to keep this information under wraps.

But maybe that's okay. Where would we be without all the jokes at the expense of our fading youth? Just walk into any Hallmark store and you'll see what I mean. I bought a card last week that said: "A word of advice on your birthday: Never stop reaching for the stars." Inside, the card added: "At least it keeps your breasts off your stomach."

We enjoy laughing at old age. It's a shade better, after all, than crying.

## When Laughter Helps the Bigger Hurts

It's one thing to yuk-it-up over crows' feet or cellulite. But sometimes we face bigger hurts that, at first glance, offer less to laugh about. Depression . . . serious illness . . . divorce . . . even death. Can we laugh? *Should* we laugh?

Sure.

In my book *Pillow Talk* I mention an experience I had with clinical depression. During those dark days, humor provided some bright moments. My sister Michelle, for example, sent me a T-shirt that sported a drawing of a cow lying flat on her back, her legs and udder pointing skyward. Not a particularly natural bovine position—and yet the shaky handwriting beneath the picture tried hard to reassure with the words: "I'm fine. *Really*." What a summary of my life at that time! Despite my feeble protests, my life wasn't okay. What was okay, however, was taking time out to crack a smile.

During the same season in my life, I received a greeting card from my sister-in-law Debbie. It asked, "Feeling depressed? Cheer up. Things could be worse . . ." Then went on to add, "You could be living in a trailer park in Yuma, wearing your bra backwards and talking to yourself." And I knew she was right: I still had reasons to count my blessings.

A friend of mine who fled a violent marriage still has flashbacks of the severe abuse. Is it any wonder that she keeps a file of funny clippings and cartoons to help her through the dark moments? She faxes samples to me now and then . . . like a whole page devoted to booger etiquette ("You can pick your friends . . . you can pick your nose . . . but you can't pick your friend's nose").

Another woman told me that she looked forward to reruns of *America's Funniest Home Videos* as a sanity-saving distraction during a season when she was caring for a dying parent.

My friend Jenny Devine manages to sport a humorous smirk despite life-threatening circumstances that no woman should have to face . . . let alone twice. Six years ago Jenny's sense of humor helped her beat breast cancer. Despite scary diagnoses, Jenny managed to find at least a small laugh at nearly every stage of her ordeal. Between tears and fears, Jenny had something humorous to say about the fact that her surgery was performed by a physician named Dr. Axe . . . about the anti-nausea medication that made her rear end itch . . . about the complications she faced because of her naturally diminutive breast size ("They can send a man to the moon. What do they mean they can't make a prosthesis small enough to match my other breast?").

> Last year Jenny developed a brain tumor. The week before having surgery to remove the tumor, she told members of her church, "On Tuesday I'm going down to the hospital and giving that doctor a piece of my mind!"

Last year, in what the doctors say is an unrelated occurrence, Jenny developed a brain tumor. The week before having surgery to remove the tumor, she told members of her church, "On Tuesday I'm going down to the hospital and giving that doctor a piece of my mind!"

Is Jenny in denial? Is she making too light of a serious topic? I don't think so. She admits to being afraid sometimes, but says that her relationship with Jesus Christ has given her an inexplicable peace about her future and the future of her husband, Jeff, and their two children, ages three and seven. Humor, she adds, lightens her perspective and helps her cope.

## Benefits of a Good Belly-Laugh

Laughter makes us feel better. And yet the benefits of a good chuckle aren't just in our minds. There is, in fact, a growing body of research pointing to a connection between laughter and our physical health as well. Laughter, for example, has been linked with enhancing our immune systems, respiratory tract, and even with the control and relief of pain.

In his book *Head First,* Norman Cousins goes as far as to compare a good belly-laugh to strenuous exercise. He explains that laughter "causes huffing and puffing, speeds up the heart rate, raises blood pressure, accelerates breathing, increases oxygen consumption, gives the muscles of the face and stomach a workout, and relaxes muscles not involved in laughing." He concludes by saying that twenty *seconds* of laughter can double the heart rate for three to five *minutes*—the same benefit reaped from three minutes of strenuous rowing (page 132).

In other words, laughter can make us healthier—in body, mind, and spirit. It releases stress, pumps up our immune system, and broadens our perspective. It can set people at ease, enhance communication, defuse squabbles. It lifts our spirits. It feels good.

Best of all, it has no calories and can't make you pregnant.

In the grand drama of family life, there's absolutely no reason why laughter shouldn't take center stage in our battle against the disappointments and setbacks that come our way.

## Humor, Hearth, and Home

How can we crank up the volume when it comes to laughter in our homes? How can we lighten up our own perspectives, and help the members of our family to do the same?

Here are a few ideas:

*Set an example.* Look for opportunities to develop and exercise your own sense of humor. Like it or not, your attitudes can set the tone for your entire family. You may have seen the plaque that warns, "If Mama ain't happy, ain't nobody happy." There's more truth to that saying than we might like to admit!

> **Laughter can make us healthier—in body, mind, and spirit. It releases stress, pumps up our immune system, enhances communication, and lifts our spirits. Best of all, it has no calories and can't make you pregnant.**

*Establish a laughter library in your home.* Collect and enjoy the efforts of other people who embrace a lighthearted perspective on life. Bookstores are filled with volumes created by talented cartoonists and humorists (my favorites are *The Far Side* cartoons by Gary Larson, and anything written by Dave Barry, Bill Cosby, or Erma Bombeck).

There may also be an actor or actress who can always make you laugh. How about Lucille Ball? Peter Sellers? Even Mel Gibson has a comedic side (and he's easy on the eyes as well!). Buy or rent videos that tickle your fancy.

Finally, you may even want to introduce notes of whimsy in the way you decorate your home. Look for coffee-table books, framed pictures, and knickknacks that arouse a smile. Photographer Anne Geddes, for example, presents a whimsical perspective of babies as flowers, butterflies, fairies, fruits, and even veggies in her magical coffee-table book *Down in the Garden.*

You can consolidate your "library" on a single shelf, or disperse these items throughout your house. The important thing is to take the time to enjoy these items with members of your family. My ten-year-old daughter and I shared a harvest of smiles browsing *Down in the Garden*. Watch funny videos together. Make a family funny album filled with cartoons clipped from newspapers or magazines, or even oddball family snapshots to which you've added crack-up captions.

*Practice humor as a way to defuse squabbles.* While you don't want to use humor as a way to avoid resolving serious conflict, sometimes smiling can provide a temporary break from mounting tensions, making resolution easier. Laughter can also provide a way out of the day-to-day silly squabbles that erupt over nothing and escalate too quickly into something.

*Without warning, grab your six-year-old and two-step across the kitchen. Use the spray nozzle at the kitchen sink to blast your fourteen-year-old as he's clearing the table. Pull your husband onto the bed for a thirty-second ticklefest.*

To teach your family how this works, you've got to be willing to model it in your own behavior. Dissolve an argument with a hug and a humorous comment. Crack a joke. Exaggerate the consequences ("I know you're frustrated with me for forgetting to pay the phone bill. What can I do to make it up to you? I know. Throw me to the lions: Let me be the one to fend off all the telephone salespeople for the next six months").

You could even make ridiculous-looking "Squabble Hats" out of construction paper and give bickering family members the choice of making up or finishing their argument while wearing the hats (this works with kids better than with husbands).

*Set aside silly time.* Occasionally set aside some silly time for your family. Have everyone come to the dinner table prepared with a new joke. Or take turns seeing who can make the funniest face or weirdest noise (you might want to set some boundaries regarding noises, particularly if you're playing this game while eating). After dinner, play a funny word game (remember Mad Libs from when we were kids?), wrestle, tell silly stories, or take a walk around the block and see who can come up with the most ridiculous gait.

*Learn the value of spontaneous funbustion.* Planned silly time is great, but don't forget to incorporate some unexpected chuckles into your day. Without warning, grab your six-year-old and two-step across the kitchen. Use the spray nozzle at the kitchen sink to blast your fourteen-year-old as he's clearing the table (just don't get mad when he retaliates in similar fashion). As your husband is putting on his tie in the morning, pull him onto the bed for a thirty-second ticklefest. In the course of the day, two or three quickies (I'm talking about quickies from the funny department; get your mind out of the gutter) will add much to your quality of life.

*Finally, make the choice to be a family of optimists.* A while ago my husband had a little talk with Kaitlyn about her attitude. He pointed out that she was developing the habit of frequently whining about one thing or another, and explained to her the difference between an optimist and a pessimist. Several days later, he pointed out to her that the whining had yet to abate. She sighed with resignation and said, "I don't know, Dad, I guess I'm just a pesticide."

We laughed at the time. But, looking back, I think her choice of words may have been more perceptive than we realize. Perhaps pessimists are a little like pesticide. After all, a pessimist can deaden a good time faster that you can say "Roach Motel." Maybe that's why we call them killjoys.

The good news is that we can choose how we are going to respond to all that life brings our way. Remember the often-told story about the glass being half-empty or half-full? Any single circumstance can be viewed from two perspectives: one negative and the other positive. Teach your kids that each of us can decide how we are going to respond to disappointment, sadness, and crisis. We can view the glass as being half-empty or half-full. We can live our lives as optimists or pesticides. The choice is ours!

"Medical researchers at a dozen or more medical centers have been probing the effects of laughter on the human body and have detailed a wide array of beneficial changes—all the way from enhanced respiration to increases in the number of disease-fighting immune cells. Extensive experiments have been conducted, working with a significant number of human beings, showing that laughter contributes to good health. Scientific evidence is accumulating to support the biblical axiom that 'a merry heart doeth good like a medicine.'" (Norman Cousins, *Head First: The Biology of Hope*, E. P. Dutton, 127)

# Family Values Can Be Found at Wal-Mart

 know all about good family values. After all, I heard Bill Bennett speak at a booksellers convention once. I've even written back-cover copy for a book on virtues. And I always vote for political candidates known to "espouse family values."

And, of course, for the ultimate in family values, I frequent Wal-Mart. And garage sales. And I clip coupons whenever I can locate the newspaper and the scissors at the same time on any given Sunday afternoon.

So I am not family-value illiterate.

And yet . . .

I can't help wondering: What exactly is a family value anyway? How is it different from a personal value? Does the phrase mean the same thing to everyone and to every group?

I asked a group of women what they thought was meant by the phrase "family values." Their answers:

"Values that cherish and nurture family life."

"Traits you want to see in your kids."

"Old-fashioned, traditional values like the ones we all grew up with."

"Values from the Bible."

However we define the phrase, everyone seemed to agree that good values—family or otherwise—include concepts such as trustworthiness, compassion, self-discipline, responsibility, respect, perseverance, loyalty, honesty, and citizenship. Things that seem foundational whether we are married or single, with or without children.

As human beings, these are the concepts we would like to have shape our lives and our choices. As parents, these are the concepts we want our children to understand and to live.

Unfortunately, this is easier said than done!

## Choose Your Values

There are literally hundreds—maybe even thousands—of values out there for us to choose from, embrace, try to exemplify, and hope to pass on to our children. It can be overwhelming! To simplify matters, let's identify some groups of values on which to focus.

Here are some examples:

William Bennett, for his book *The Book of Virtues,* chose the following ten traits to highlight above the rest: self-discipline, compassion, responsibility, friendship, work, courage, perseverance, honesty, loyalty, and faith.

Character Counts!, a program that promotes character education in public schools, teaches students about the "Six Pillars" of character, defined as trustworthiness, respect, responsibility, fairness, caring, and citizenship.

217

*Teaching values to our children works best when we honor an uncomfortable and annoying rule of thumb: We need to practice what we preach.*

The Bible says that the life of someone truly in tune with God's own Spirit will exemplify the following nine characteristics: love, joy, peace, patience, kindness, goodness, faithfulness, gentleness, and self-control.

By identifying a half-dozen-or-so values that you consider to be of great priority, you aren't saying that you'll never strive to incorporate the others into your life. But if you never prioritize—if you never focus on a select few at a time—the chances are slim that you will ever master any.

Do you have your list? If not, put this book down and create one, identifying a handful of values that you deem more significant than any others.

## Practice What You Preach

Our goal as adults, parents, and architects of our families is to empower our children with the values they'll need to succeed in this life and on into eternity.

I wish I could do this with my words. Unfortunately, my actions shout so loudly, my kids usually can't hear what I'm saying with my mouth. Indeed, teaching values to our children works best when we honor an uncomfortable and annoying rule of thumb: We need to practice what we preach.

My husband tells a story that took place during his childhood. I've been married to Larry sixteen years, and I've heard this story that many times or more. It goes like this:

When Larry was a teenager, he and his brother, Chris, went with their dad to the ballpark on a humid summer day to watch their team play. While waiting in line to purchase tickets, they befriended a Boy Scout leader accompanied by about a dozen Scouts. When the Scout leader discovered that Larry and Chris were Eagle Scouts and that Dad was, indeed, a Scout leader himself, he made a proposal: "Join our group and help me supervise these boys. You're legitimately a Scout leader, I sure could use the help, and—as a chaperone—the ballpark will let you in free of charge."

Dad, who is a helpful sort of guy and frugal-minded as well, agreed to the plan, which most of us would consider well within the boundaries of ethical behavior. And yet, in his heart of hearts, Dad felt he had entered the ballpark under false pretenses. He was dogged by the nagging thought that he had misrepresented himself in order to save six bucks.

*Kids are pretty sharp. Early on in their short lives they develop this healthy aversion to being asked to do something that their parents are unwilling to do themselves.*

Four years later, he wrote a letter of apology to the ballpark and enclosed a check for six dollars. The check was returned uncashed, with a note from the park administration expressing their thanks and assuring Dad that his assistance with the troop was well worth the price of his admission. But, of course, whether the check was cashed or not was academic to the teenage boy who observed the whole thing and internalized something about honesty and integrity in the process.

If you've flown commercially, you are acquainted with the emergency-procedures spiel that flight attendants pantomime at the beginning of every flight: The seat cushions will float . . . emergency exits are here, here, and here . . . the oxygen mask will drop like so . . .

And if you've flown with a small child, you may have noticed the part about securing your oxygen mask before you turn to help your children in case of an emergency.

Before I became a parent, that seemed like odd advice. But now that I'm a mother, it's making more and more sense all the time. Kids are pretty sharp. Early on in their short lives they develop this healthy aversion to being asked to do something that their parents are unwilling to do themselves. It applies to oxygen masks. And it applies to our values.

I had a chance to put this concept into practice just the other night. While cooking dinner, I grabbed the carton of Morton salt and gave it a fast shake over the potatoes frying on the stove, careful to keep too much salt from escaping from the spout. Setting the salt on the stove, I moved toward the sink, looking back in time to see my ten-year-old grab the container and—just like Mom—give it the ol' one-two over the potatoes.

I blew my top. Convinced dinner was ruined, I scolded and yelled. When Kaitlyn stormed, angry and hurt, to her room, it dawned on me that I had overreacted. Sure, I needed to say something. But I didn't need to wound her in the process.

I knew I needed to apologize. I considered going to Kaitlyn's room to do it. And then something dawned on me. When Kaitlyn explodes publicly—in front of family or friends—I encourage her to apologize in the same environment in which the offense took place. While I don't think apologies need to be flaunted, I figure that if we're not embarrassed to act badly in front of other people, we shouldn't be embarrassed to apologize in front of that same group.

I had embarrassed Kaitlyn in the kitchen, undoubtedly within earshot of Diane, a college student staying at our house for a semester. My apology needed to be just as public.

I called Kaitlyn into the kitchen, pulled her onto my lap, and began practicing what I so often preach: "Kaitlyn, I overreacted. I needed to say something to you, but I was wrong to yell at you like I did, and I'm sorry I did that. Will you forgive me?" She said yes with a grin and a hug. Later, we talked about the old saying that too many cooks spoil the broth. I fished the saltiest potatoes out of the pan and dinner was saved. So was peace in the family.

Practice what you preach. It's the best way to teach . . . and not a bad way to live, either.

*It's possible to reframe morality so many times that, before long, nothing is recognizable anymore.*

## A Picture Is Worth a Thousand Words

Sometimes talking about compassion or perseverance or faithfulness can seem nebulous to a child without a concrete example. Let actions provide examples of virtues you want your child to emulate.

When you see your child demonstrating a positive trait, point it out. Last week Kacie took a tumble from a chair and ended up on the kitchen floor, crying. Before I could reach her, Kaitlyn had sped to her sister's side and scooped her into a comforting hug. After a couple hiccups, Kacie settled into her sister's arms. It would be easy for me to thank Kaitlyn for helping her sister; how much better if I used the opportunity to link her action with a specific virtue such as compassion. I could say, "Thank you, Kaitlyn, for showing *compassion* to Kacie."

The same thing applies to the actions of others. If I clip coupons, I can point out to my kids the benefit of being *thrifty.* If Dad takes a day from work for jury duty, I can use the word *citizenship* in connection with his actions. When my friend Nancy Rottmeyer helped me wallpaper the kitchen, I told my kids how *teamwork* made the job so much easier!

By the same token, correctly label negative behaviors as well. If your son asks you to tell a peer he's not home when he is, in fact, hiding in his room, tell him, "That's lying. We don't lie."

So often the world sends distorted messages about the meaning of things: Sleeping with a married man isn't adultery, it's finding true love despite inconvenient circumstances. Abortion isn't ending a life, it's emptying a uterus. Telling your boss you're sick when you're not isn't lying, it's beating the system. Going off the deep end and killing someone isn't about murder, but about being driven by your own feelings of victimization. It's possible to reframe morality so many times that, before long, nothing is recognizable anymore. To combat this in your own home, use the words. Attach them to actions. Help your kids understand what lying looks like. And envy. And greed. And, in the same light, what honesty looks like. And patience. And compassion.

## Bring Values to the Forefront in Creative Fashions

Help your children to embrace good values by under-scoring positive values in creative ways. Here are a couple of ideas.

Select a value of the month and plan several ways to celebrate that virtue throughout the month. Take charity, for example. You could spend a Saturday morning with your kids providing services for an elderly or house-bound member of your church or neighborhood: make a casserole, mow the lawn, vacuum the house. You might also encourage your kids to clip newspaper or magazine articles that illustrate charity. The person who finds the most articles by the end of the month gets to pick the restaurant for a family dinner on the town. Write a poem about charity, cut out magazine pictures and make a collage, or nominate family members for an "Act of Charity" Award.

A public school in Franklin, Massachusetts, has created a "Forest of Virtues" in the foyer of their building. Peg Murphy, the school's founder, explains: "There are four paper tree trunks, representing prudence, justice, fortitude, and temperance—what the ancient Greeks called the cardinal virtues." As students observe someone in the school community modeling one of the virtues, they nominate their name to be written on a leaf. At the end of each week, the leaves are placed on the trees.

Keep a family values journal. Create a loose-leaf notebook with a divider for each of the seven (or ten, or twelve) values on which you hope to focus as a family. When a family member does something that exemplifies that value, write a paragraph about it and put it in the notebook. Other things you could put in your notebook: Bible verses, photographs, thank-you notes, ribbons or awards received in conjunction with a particular value (for example, place a child's Honor Roll Certificate in the section marked "Diligence," or the thank-you note received for raking a neighbor's yard in the section marked "Kindness").

## Pay the Price

One friend pointed out that values are valuable because they cost us something. How true! If we aren't willing to pay a price to live by any given principle, it's not really a value that we hold dear.

If I say honesty is important, but I'm never willing to pay a price for being honest, then I'm fooling myself.

If I say charity is a priority, but I am only willing to help someone else when it is convenient and my own comfort is not compromised, then charity is not something I truly value.

If I think perseverance is a good trait, and yet I persevere only until I get tired or bored or distracted, then I'd better re-think what is truly important to me.

Talk to your kids about the price that is often exacted when we choose to live by high standards. Let them know the price you've paid for right choices you've made in your life. Help them understand that they, too, will have to pay a toll in order to live by certain values.

As I was growing up, my dad owned his own printing company. As with any business, sometimes cash flow was tight. During one such time, my dad received a call from a company looking for someone to handle a four-color printing job. The money was good, the deadline was reasonable, and the man on the phone seemed genuinely thrilled to have my dad consider the job. My dad, of course, was even happier. This job was an answer to prayer.

The next day, my dad drove to the company's headquarters to finalize negotiations. When he did, he was handed the photographs he was expected to print . . . and discovered they were nothing less than pornography. My dad refused the job. The man doubled the money. Then tripled it. My dad walked away.

His values cost him something. But he was willing to pay the price because, in the end, he knew he was hanging onto something that money couldn't buy.

We live in a time when convenience and comfort have been elevated to godlike stature. Remember that good family values don't come cheap. They're not always convenient. And they may not increase our comfort level. But they're worth the price we pay.

Be willing to pay the price. Teach your kids to do the same. It's an investment that will reap dividends in the end.

## Reap the Reward

Just as we want our children to understand that living according to high standards will require something from us, they need to understand that living lawlessly exacts a much heavier toll.

We are daily exposed to stories and situations that reflect the ramifications of a life lived without boundaries or solid values. Use these situations to point out to your kids the price of unhealthy choices:

224

- If your daughter's classmate drops out of tenth grade to have a baby, use the opportunity to talk about the value of abstinence and the heavy price that may be paid when that principle is thrown to the wind.
- If a relative dies in mid-life due to lung cancer brought on by decades of smoking, talk about the price that is paid when self-control is ignored.
- If your son suffers a broken heart when his best friend steals his girlfriend, there may be an opportunity to talk about the value of loyalty and the damage that is done when loyalty takes a backseat to selfishness.

At the same time . . .

Virtuous living isn't just about paying a price . . . and trying to avoid paying the even greater price that comes with selfish choices.

Virtuous living is rich with rewards. Look for opportunities to talk about these, as well:

- When you celebrate the fiftieth wedding anniversary of a grandparent or friend, point out to your children the rich rewards of fidelity and commitment in marriage.
- When a promotion at work means financial benefit for your family, talk about the rewards of hard work and diligence.
- When a teenager you know scrimped and saved and ended up buying a nicer car than his spendthrift friends, talk about the values of patience and wise spending.

Two nights ago there was a flurry of excitement in my home. Diane, the college friend I mentioned earlier who is living with my family for a semester, flew in the front door in a giddy whirl, an engagement ring sparkling on her left hand.

Diane and her fiancé stayed long enough to show us her ring, toast their engagement with a glass of sparkling apple juice, and call her parents to announce their news and say they'd be over as soon as they could make the thirty-mile drive.

When they arrived at Diane's childhood home, they were amazed to discover that an impromptu engagement party was already in full swing. Diane's parents, sisters, brother-in-law, best friend, and her pastor and his wife had spontaneously convened out of sheer joy for this young Christian couple.

*When a teenager you know scrimped and saved and ended up buying a nicer car than his spendthrift friends, use the opportunity to talk to your kids about the values of patience and wise spending.*

In fact, everyone who knows Diane and Hector is thrilled at their announcement. They seem a match made in heaven.

Kaitlyn, of course, is enthralled. Romance, diamonds, bride's magazines, and wedding plans—intoxicating stuff, even to a ten-year-old. And, naturally, I can't pass up the opportunity to talk with her about the kind of values Diane and Hector embraced that got them to this happy moment: They met at church, they dated over a period of years, they valued the wisdom and input of their parents, they stayed sexually pure, they sought counsel from their pastor before becoming engaged. And their reward? Well, that's easy enough to spot in their eyes and in the happy congratulations of those who know them best.

Family values. They don't come cheap, but they pay off in the end. When it comes to teaching your kids about values, the best thing you can do is talk the talk and walk the walk. Of course, it doesn't always come easy . . . but if you're consistent, your children will not only learn about values, they'll know they are valued as well.

 ### Prioritize Your Values

William Bennett, for his book *The Book of Virtues*, chose the following ten traits to highlight above the rest: self-discipline, compassion, responsibility, friendship, work, courage, perseverance, honesty, loyalty, and faith.

Character Counts!, a program that promotes character education in public schools, teaches students about the "Six Pillars" of character: trustworthiness, respect, responsibility, fairness, caring, and citizenship.

The Bible says that the life of someone truly in tune with God's own Spirit will exemplify the following nine characteristics: love, joy, peace, patience, kindness, goodness, faithfulness, gentleness, and self-control.

By identifying a half-dozen or so values that you consider to be of great priority, you aren't saying that you'll never strive to incorporate the others into your life. But if you never prioritize—if you never focus on a select few at a time—the chances are slim that you'll ever master any.

# Imitation Is the Sincerest Form of Flattery

**W**ould someone please tell me why children can't seem to make up their minds on one particularly vital issue? I am referring, of course, to the matter of example. Life would be so much easier if our kids could live by one simple policy, either following our examples all of the time, or none of the time. I wouldn't even care which one they chose, as long as they stayed consistent.

As it stands, kids have the truly irritating habit of ignoring us when we are trying to teach them something we want them to know, and following our examples when we are sneaking around trying to hide an embarrassing flaw or nasty habit.

We tried for months to teach Kacie to say Daddy. When she was thirteen months old she had mastered Mama, Doo-doo (for Sister), and dawgie. The word that children often learn first, and Kacie refused to learn at all, was Daddy.

But it's not like she didn't have a name for him. She called him Mom. For months. Which was not a real big ego booster for my husband.

Every evening when she heard her dad unlocking the front door, Kacie would drop whatever she was doing and race to the front hall, arms outstretched in anticipation of a hug, face shining, and all the while calling, "Mom! Mom!"

Larry and I tried in vain to correct her. And then, one night, there was a turning point. I remember lying on my stomach on the bed in our room, watching Larry assemble a Sit-Up Master on the floor. In his lap, hindering the entire process but doing it in a truly adorable way, was Kacie. At one point, I heard Larry say, "See, Kacie? Mom's working hard," and I knew he was making fun of me because obviously I was *not* working hard: I hadn't moved for twenty minutes. Then he added, "See, Kacie, Mom's using the screwdriver. This is a screwdriver, Kacie." And I realized he wasn't talking about me at all.

*They say imitation is the sincerest form of flattery. And yet it's not flattering at all when you see your precious offspring latch on to your worst characteristics like a pit bull on a mail carrier.*

Yes, there was a turning point—for Larry—and it happened the night he gave in and became "Mom."

Of course, it was perhaps a month later that Kacie surprised us all by saying "Daddy." But it was on her time line, not ours. And in the process we were reminded, once again, that sometimes kids have their own ideas about what to imitate and what to ignore.

## Is It Real? Or Is It Memorex?

When our children aren't busy ignoring what we tell them to do, they are usually doing one of two things. The first thing that they do is reflect back to us things we were hoping they hadn't even noticed.

They say imitation is the sincerest form of flattery. And yet it's not flattering at all when you see your precious offspring latch on to your worst characteristics like a pit bull on a mail carrier. Maybe it's an attitude that is distasteful or even damaging, such as apathy toward spiritual things, bitterness toward an ex-spouse, perfectionism, anger, or pessimism.

It might be a habit that you wish you could kick: watching too much TV, gossiping about friends or family, unhealthy eating, or even some sort of substance abuse.

Did you ever watch the TV show *thirtysomething*? I did. Actually, I was a *thirtysomething* junkie. I thought I'd need therapy when Gary died. I still have dreams about running into Melissa at a party, exchanging hugs and saying, "So, how *is* everybody? Give me all the news." But I guess all that's a confession for another book. What I really wanted to say is that I remember one episode in which TV-mom Hope Steadman becomes puzzled over perfectionism in her three-year-old: Janie's preschool teacher notices the child getting overly upset when she colors outside the lines. Before the hour ends, Hope discovers the genesis of Janie's obsession with perfection, and—you guessed it—it's Hope. Obsessing over a birthday party for her husband, Hope learns the hard way that "You can be right. Or you can be happy." Later, Hope confesses to her sleeping daughter, "You learned everything well. Too well. You learned things I never meant to teach you . . ."

That's my lament too. It might even be yours. So what can we do about it? What do we do when our children learn too well? When they end up catching on to things we never meant for them to learn?

It would be great if we could handle this dilemma by simply shaping up—either becoming perfect or being able to consistently appear perfect when little eyes are watching! The problem with either of these solutions is that they are unlikely to occur in our lifetime. In fact, we have better odds of winning the lottery, getting a good parking spot at the mall the day after Thanksgiving, or standing on our bathroom scales and realizing we've dropped fifteen pounds without even trying.

*Are you prone to gossip? Be honest with your kids. Talk to them about some of the times you've hurt a friend or been embarrassed by something that you've said.*

In fact, if we try this approach—if we say to ourselves, "My kids are prone to mimic my flaws, therefore I must try to appear perfect at all times"—pretty soon we'll look at our kids, observe perfectionism, hypocrisy, or denial, and wonder where in the world they learned *these* things!

The bad news is that we can't hide our sins from our kids. The good news is that this isn't all bad. If our kids are able to observe our flaws, they're also in prime position to observe how we deal with those flaws.

And how do we deal with our flaws? Do we get defensive? Are we queens of denial? Are we always looking for a scapegoat? Do we blame our past or our parents or our husbands or the time of the month? Does our imperfection drive us toward destructive coping mechanisms such as compulsive spending or eating, drinking, or depression?

Or do we deal with our flaws with integrity, strength, and hope? Can we admit when we've made a mistake? Are we willing to ask for help when we need it? Are we honest with ourselves about our shortcomings? Is self-improvement something that matters to us? Are we accountable for our choices . . . even the bad ones?

Maybe watching our mistakes—and watching how we correct and learn from our mistakes—our kids will be somehow better prepared for the inevitable failings that await them in their own lives.

Are you prone to gossip? Be honest with your kids. Let them know this is a form of communication that can be damaging. Talk to them about some of the times you've hurt a friend or been embarrassed by something that you've said. Ask your kids to pray and encourage you as you try to learn healthier communication patterns.

Are there unhealthy habits in your life? Smoking, overeating, or a sedentary lifestyle are health risks you don't want to pass along to your kids. Make the effort to develop new lifestyle patterns. As your family witnesses your struggle and—hopefully—your eventual success, they'll be learning important lessons about things like perseverance and self-control. Who knows? They may even catch on to the fact that it's easier to develop wise habits in the first place than to try to relearn bad ones!

Any way we look at it, kids learn from our mistakes. If all they see are our mistakes, they may follow in our footsteps and make the same ones. If they see our mistakes—and also observe the repentance, integrity, and character with which we respond to our mistakes—then the learning that takes place just might not be a bad thing after all! Indeed, our children just might end up internalizing some pretty powerful principles in the process.

## Will They Remember What I Did Right?

It's scary to think that the young people in our homes are watching our every move and determining which part of our lives to internalize and imitate. And yet, there's an upside to all this.

Sometimes they actually catch on to something we did right.

Friends Bill and Linda Yarbrough tell the story of the Sunday afternoon their hearts sank as they realized their son, away at college, had been drinking the night before. They were on the phone, chatting with Craig about his classes, friends, and dating life, when they realized he wasn't his usual chipper self. Craig admitted that he had gone partying with friends the night before, and that for the first time, he hadn't been the designated driver.

Bill and Linda worried that a single night of indiscretion would become a destructive pattern in their son's life. But it never happened. Craig never drank again.

Several years later, Craig explained why.

*The lives we lead as parents are paving the way, blazing the trail, illuminating the footpath for the precious ones that follow.*

"After my first hangover, I did a lot of thinking. On one hand, it was fun to party with the guys and feel cool and tough. But then I thought about my dad. He's the toughest guy I know. He's a man's man for sure. And it dawned on me that I've never seen him drink. Not one time. Not ever. If he didn't need it, neither did I. I knew right then that I'd never drink again."

Wouldn't it be nice to know what lessons and insights our children will take with them from our homes? I know that, personally, I would sleep easier at night knowing that, somewhere down the line, my commitment to my marriage will inspire Kaitlyn to do the same . . . or my dedication to my writing will encourage Kacie as she pursues her gifts and dreams . . . or that our faith in God will provide a beacon for our girls as they test and define their own belief system.

Yeah, that would be nice. But in a way, I already know. They're watching it all. It all matters. There are no guarantees, of course, but the lives we lead as parents are paving the way, blazing the trail, illuminating the footpath for the precious ones that follow. In the very end, our kids will have to choose. Will they imitate what we lived? Or will they make a different choice? No matter what, I want my life to have painted a picture that's crystal clear. It won't be a picture of perfection, that's for sure. But that's okay. As long as I'm willing to learn from my mistakes, maybe my kids will be, too.

## Myth #20

# Sticks and Stones May Break My Bones, but Words Will Never Hurt Me

ommunication among family members is a strange and wonderful thing. And so varied, too! Just think about all the possibilities: Lipstick messages on bathroom mirrors . . . notes on paper napkins in school lunches . . . a sigh of contentment or exasperation . . . the push or shove of an agitated toddler . . . facial configurations that would make Jim Carrey or Bill Cosby proud . . . icy tones . . . warm laughter . . . rolling eyeballs . . . a subtle wink . . . and the message that comes rolled up in a big bear hug.

And then there are words. Words pretty much fall into two categories: the ones you want to hear, and the ones you don't want to hear. Words you want to hear from family members are things like: "I love you," "How about dinner out tonight?" and "Please, *please, please* can I do the dishes this week?"

Words you don't want to hear include: "Honey, I just opened the credit card bill and there's this huge charge . . . I'm sure it must be a mistake . . ." and "Mom, um . . . do you remember your favorite necklace with the broken clasp that you told me not to borrow until you got it fixed?" or "Mom, Dad, I'd like you to meet my boyfriend. I'll bring him by as soon as he's out on parole."

> *Somewhere we've gotten this idea that words aren't that important. But I just can't agree. Sticks and stones, after all, never sent anyone into therapy.*

Somewhere we've gotten this idea that words aren't that important. We've all heard, "Sticks and stones may break my bones, but words can never hurt me." But I just can't agree. Sticks and stones, after all, never sent anyone into therapy.

No, our words carry more weight than any one of us can imagine. Words have power. If I didn't believe that, I wouldn't have become a writer.

How much power do words have?

Words have so much power that companies will pay hundreds of thousands of dollars to tell you about their product for a mere thirty seconds on Superbowl Sunday.

Words have so much power that God used them to create the world and the universe, the fish and the fowl, lions and tigers and bears (oh my!), and man and woman, too.

Words have so much power that the longing for words of affirmation will send grown men and women into an emotional tailspin; and harsh, demeaning words will leave children with crippled spirits for life.

Listen to what the Bible has to say about the power of our words:

If anyone can control his tongue, it proves that he has perfect control over himself in every other way. We can make a large horse turn around and go wherever we want by means of a small bit in his mouth. And a tiny rudder makes a huge ship turn wherever the pilot wants it to go, even though the winds are strong.

So also the tongue is a small thing, but what enormous damage it can do. A great forest can be set on fire by one tiny spark. And the tongue is a flame of fire. It . . . can turn our whole life into a blazing flame of destruction and disaster.

James 3:2–6 TLB

Words can hurt. And demean. And destroy. They can also salve and stroke and encourage. How can we harness this power to benefit, not harm, the members of our families? How can we teach our kids that their words have power to heal or to hurt?

## What to Say When Words Leave Wounds

When our youngsters come to us smarting from the insensitive words of a playmate, what do we say to them? If you're like me, your first reaction is to belittle the words of the taunter:

"He's just making noise. Ignore him."
"She didn't mean that."

"Those are just words."

"What does he know? Don't listen to him."

Does this approach make our kids feel any better? Maybe. Maybe not. But what are we teaching them about the importance of words? If rude comments received shouldn't matter, then rude comments given shouldn't matter, either! Later, when our kids are the ones spouting the wounding phrases, we'll wonder why they don't realize the power of their words.

Perhaps a better response would be to acknowledge that, yes, words can hurt . . . big time! Perhaps we would do well to talk about the pain that harsh words can cause, saying something like:

> "I'm sorry she said that to you. I can see that her words really hurt your feelings."
>
> "Those seem like harsh words. I can understand why you're angry."
>
> "I can see that his words had a big impact on you. How did they make you feel inside?"

This approach does a couple of things:

First, it establishes the fact that, indeed, words are capable of stinging and causing pain.

Second, when we identify the emotions—such as anger, sadness, rejection—that our kids are exhibiting in response to their pain, it helps them learn to recognize and give names to their feelings, an important skill for good emotional health.

Finally, this approach opens the door for further communication with our kids. When we belittle their pain by saying things like, "Those are just words. Ignore them," we are shutting down communication. We're saying, in effect, "Get over it. Case closed." On the other hand, if our kids realize that we understand their pain, they may feel secure enough to talk further about the situation. If this is the case, in the ensuing conversation, look for ways to introduce some healing and/or teaching concepts. Here are some ideas:

"Honey, lots of times people don't realize how powerful their words can be. My guess is that Susan didn't mean to hurt you, just as I know you didn't mean to hurt your brother when you spoke harshly to him yesterday in the car. Do you think you can give Susan the benefit of the doubt and forgive her for her thoughtless comment?"

"It sounds as though by belittling you, Josh was trying to build himself up in front of his friends. I wonder why he felt he needed to do that? What could he have been feeling inside? Do you think maybe he was nervous or afraid and this was his way of hiding those feelings?"

"You and Jennifer have been friends for a long time. My guess is that your friendship is as important to Jennifer as it is to you. Have you told her that the nickname really bothers you and asked her not to use it anymore? Until you do that, it's unfair to be mad at her. She may not even know it bothers you!"

"It hurts to learn that someone doesn't like you. I wish I could protect you forever from this kind of feeling! But the truth is that you will have this feeling many times in your life. This is because no one person in the entire world is liked by everyone. Even Jesus had people who hated him. There are people who don't like your dad and me. Even your favorite Uncle Joe has enemies! You may never know why Aimie doesn't like you: maybe you remind her of someone who hurt her feelings once . . . maybe her parents yelled at her this morning and she was looking for someone to belittle this af-

> *Sometimes it's enough to tell our children, "I know you're hurting and I wish I could take away the pain . . ." and hold them long and hard, sharing their tears.*

ternoon . . . maybe she doesn't like the way you wore your hair last week . . . maybe she loves the way you wear your hair and she's trying to hurt you because she's jealous. You may never understand. All I know is that Aimie is missing out on something great by not wanting to be friends with you. I actually feel sorry for her. Maybe we should add her to our prayers tonight. Let's ask God to bless Aimie and let her find some good friends who can help her understand the importance of friendship and how important it is not to judge people or put them down."

For the deepest hurts, words—as powerful as they are—may fall short of providing the right lesson, insight, or comfort. Sometimes it's enough to tell our children, "I know you're hurting and I wish I could take away the pain . . ." and hold them long and hard, sharing their tears.

Words can hurt. We do our children a disservice to let them grow up believing anything less.

## The Healing Power of Words

There are lots of things I want my daughters to learn before they leave my home. One of them is that, just as their words have the power to hurt, they have the power to heal as well. Wouldn't it be great if you and I made a conscious effort to teach our kids the art of positive communication? Just for a moment, think about all the different types of communication that build self-esteem, confirm a positive truth, or bestow a warm-fuzzy! Here are twelve forms of positive communication that deserve a prime place in our homes:

*Compliment* ("What a pretty dress you're wearing!")

*Appreciation* ("Thank you for making dinner tonight. I know it takes time, and your efforts don't go unnoticed!")

*Thank-you note* ("Thanks, Gramma, for the birthday card and money.")

*Admiration* ("Something that I've always admired about you, Aunt Shelly, is the way you treat me just like a grown-up when we're together!")

*Recognition of accomplishment* ("Congratulations on making the A/B Honor Roll at school. I know that takes a lot of hard work. You deserve to be proud of your efforts.")

*Birthday greetings* ("I didn't know what to get you so I called the Birthday Hotline . . . You know, 1-900-Over-The-Hill! Happy Birthday Anyway!")

*Affirmation* ("I'm glad you're my sister because . . .")

*Encouragement* ("Mom, I know this has been a hectic week for you at the office. I just wanted you to know I love you and I'm thinking about you.")

*Expression of pride* ("Dad, I'm proud of you because . . .")

*Get-well wishes* ("Dear Pastor Snowden, I heard on Sunday that you were home with the flu. I hope you're feeling better soon and that you'll be able to be back at church next week.")

*Counting blessings* ("I just wanted to tell you about a neat thing that happened to me today.")

*Telling someone about your faith* ("Todd, I don't know how you feel about 'religion,' but I'm a Christian, and here's why my relationship with Jesus is important to me . . ." or "You're right, Ashley, breaking up with John was really hard for me to do. But I knew it was the right decision, and my relationship with Jesus gave me the courage to do it . . ." or "Michael, I know you're worried about your dad losing his job. If you don't mind, I'd like to pray about it. You don't have to pray out loud or anything. You can just listen. Dear Jesus . . .")

What would happen if you and I called family meetings in our homes and established the goal of practicing these "communication forms" on a daily basis? Perhaps we could encourage our spouses and kids to select one communication style from the list each day and put it into practice—and, of course, you and I would need to practice what we preach! Maybe we could post these twelve techniques on the refrigerator and refer to them often. We could keep a box of greeting cards, note cards, stamps, and addresses visible for easy access. We might even create a chart for family members to draw a check mark or smiley face on the days they met the goal.

*When I was growing up, my grandfather nicknamed everyone in my family. My name—oh, this is so embarrassing—was "Moogie." Actually, Papaw called me "Moog" for short.*

How might the atmosphere in our homes be transformed? I wish I could say that I've been practicing these ideas with my family for the past three years, and that I have two golden-tongued children as a result. What I can do, however, is promise that I'm willing to give it a try if you are! Let's meet with our families this week and establish guidelines. Let's practice godly communication in our homes. You can write to me and let me know how it's working for you, and I'll let you know in my next book how it's working for me!

## But You Can Call Me Scooter

Why is it so tempting to call each other anything and everything besides our actual given names? For some reason, family life creates an environment ripe for pet names, nicknames, humorous labels, and funny stereotyping. When I was growing up, my grandfather nicknamed everyone in my family. He called my dad "Spud" (his name is Gene), my mom "Sweetie," my aunt Jeanette "Trick." My sister Michelle became "Pete," my cousin Michael was called "Gabe," and my name . . . oh, this is so embarrassing . . . my name was "Moogie." Actually, Papaw called me "Moog" for short.

*Avoid stereotyping one child as "the smart one," or "the brains in the family," which might leave siblings feeling as though they got the leftovers from the family gene pool.*

For years, my dad called one of my sisters "Tiger" in honor of her feisty, no-nonsense attitude. When Renee was in her teens my mom, weary of battling her strong-willed daughter, wondered if the nickname hadn't promoted the very characteristic it was designed to merely reflect. Hoping to defuse the intensity with which Renee approached all of life, my mom gave her a new nickname: "Lambie." It was always a bit of a misnomer: You might say my go-getter sister remained a tiger in sheep's clothing.

Nicknames can be endearing. Comforting. They can create an intimate bond between family members.

But if we're not careful, the nicknames intended for fun can cause secret wounds and hidden pain. Derogatory names, or names that poke fun or stereotype a child in a negative way, need to be avoided no matter what! That means nix the "Blondie," "Slowpoke," "Airhead," "Butterball," and "Stringbean," no matter how lovingly they are used! Also, avoid stereotyping one child as "the smart one," or "the brains in the family," which might leave siblings feeling as though they got the leftovers from the family gene pool.

Our words are undoubtedly one of our greatest resources when it comes to shaping, affirming, teaching, and connecting with our children. Believe it or not, the same children who seem incapable of hearing any sentence beginning with the words "I want you to . . ." are, in reality, listening and internalizing most of what we're saying!

Just last night I said to my toddler, "Sweetie, come here and let me tie your shoe," and my ten-year-old responded, "My shoe *is* tied." When I explained that I was talking to her sister, Kaitlyn seemed dismayed. "But *I'm* your 'Sweetie.' You can't call her sweetie, that's what you call me. That's *my* name. Come up with something else for her!"

Our kids *are* listening. Words do make a difference. Let's choose ours carefully.

 ## 31 Ways to Praise Your Child

| | |
|---|---|
| Way to go! | Nice going! |
| I love you. | You've improved so much. |
| Good job. | I'm proud of you. |
| You're my sunshine. | You're a winner. |
| Wow! | I'm so lucky to be your mom. |
| You're special. | You bring me such joy. |
| Great! | What a good idea. |
| I missed you today. | You're terrific. |
| Sensational! | I'm so glad you're you. |

You make me happy.

You brighten my day.

You did it!

I thank God for you every day.

Very nice.

That's so neat.

Wonderful!

Cool.

Awesome.

You did great.

You're the apple of my eye.

How nice to see your smiling face!

I'm impressed.

# Rules Are Made to Be Broken

 like rules about as much as I like rope burns.

Recently I was preparing to make macaroni and cheese when my friend Cherie walked over from next door. She observed me for a moment and then said, "You're supposed to boil the water before putting the noodles in."

I looked down at my noodles sitting in cold water. "No kidding? I didn't know that."

"It says so right on the box, in the directions."

"Really? There are directions?"

Is this scary to anyone else but me? Here I am, a thirty-six-year-old mom who has been feeding Kraft macaroni and cheese to her children since the mid '80s and I didn't know they came with directions—the macaroni, not the children. Children *definitely* don't come with directions.

246

Then again, even if I had known there were directions on the box, would I have read them? Probably not. Rules and me . . . well, let's just say we're acquaintances. We nod at each other now and then as we pass in the corridors of life. Katherine Hepburn once observed, "If you obey all the rules, you miss all the fun," and I happen to think she just might be right! There is, however, a downside to structureless living. The truth is that I find myself confronted daily with challenges that a more organized, rule-driven person would never dream of experiencing. Indeed, keeping track of basic life tools such as keys, checkbook, contact lenses, and even my cordless phone seems, at times, more than I can handle.

Several weeks ago I found myself standing on my front porch, keys in hand, trying to unlock my front door when it dawned on me that my house key was not on the ring. Just before I began to panic, my ten-year-old announced, "Oh! I forgot! I have your key," and produced it from her jacket pocket. She had been playing with my keys during church, and thought I knew she'd taken one of them off the ring.

I was upset, and rightfully so. But what struck me as odd was the fact that I was not just upset, I was shaken. In fact, my family was surprised by how unnerved I was over the incident, and so was I!

Thinking deeply about my reaction, I finally figured it out. Because I'm not an organized person, I have to work really hard at making sure I have everything in working order, meaning keys where I need them, checkbook where I can find it, head screwed on straight . . . As it is, I sabotage my own efforts frequently enough; to have my efforts so easily undone in such a manner by someone else, well . . . to tell the truth, it scared me!

Sometimes I try to get control of my life by establishing the very thing I'm hoping to avoid: Rules. In fact, I establish rules all the time. I create charts and graphs and checklists and diagrams. The thing I can't seem to do is give a wooden nickel for any of them five minutes after they've been created.

Just this morning I was awakened by a pair of sneakers being planted on my chest. I blinked. "What's this?"

"Just helping you with your new rule," Larry said good-naturedly from the closet where he was conducting an extensive manhunt for a clean shirt.

"What rule?"

"Two days ago you said that no one was allowed to leave any room of the house without first asking, 'Is anything out of place in this room?' and if so, putting the stray item away. Your shoes were in the bathroom this morning. I'm helping you put them away."

"I think *you* were supposed to put them away. And, for the record, they're supposed to go in the closet, not on your wife," I said. "That's how the rule is supposed to work."

"I think the rule is that anyone still in bed on a Tuesday morning who makes rules on Sunday and forgets them by Monday must be aroused from slumber by the careful placement of sneakers on body parts to be selected by her husband, particularly if he finds said sneakers while searching in vain for clean white dress shirts that appear (a) not to exist or (b) to have been abducted by aliens who spend their weekends impersonating Mormon missionaries."

I could see that this rule business was getting us nowhere, and at the speed of light, no less.

"Nano, nano," I said, and went back to sleep.

## Foolproof Family Rules

Sometimes I get the urge to create a family rule that, one month later, will still be intact. Unbroken. Uncompromised by the "catch-can" nature of life in the busy '90s. It's a confidence booster to be able to say that, indeed, there are certain rules in my family that, due to steely powers of determination and self-control, have never been crossed. Not once.

Family rules that fall into this category include the rule that states that no conventions attended by Elvis impersonators will be allowed to convene in our home during any month that ends with the letter "y."

Or the rule that says that plastic surgery is not an acceptable science project for my children, regardless of what their peers are doing or how many chins their mother may have.

Or the rule that says that pets must weigh less than the family van. They also cannot snack on neighborhood children, list "Jurassic Park" as their previous address, or answer to the nickname "Rex."

Obviously, the key to establishing realistic family rules is to set goals that are attainable.

This same principle also takes the stress out of New Year's resolutions. The key, once again, is to make your resolution attainable. With a little foresight you too can wow your friends in April by announcing that you have honored your New Year's resolution for four whole months with a flawless fervency even Gandhi would have admired. It is entirely up to you to decide if you want to tell them the nature of your resolution.

*It's a confidence-booster to be able to say that, indeed, there are certain rules in my family that have never been crossed. Not once. Family rules that fall into this category include the rule that no conventions attended by Elvis impersonators will be allowed to convene in our home during any month that ends with the letter "y."*

For the least stress and greatest chance of success, consider resolutions such as, "I promise to air out the sheets on my bed by leaving it unmade whenever I am running late to work," or "I promise to reduce my intake of sugar and fat whenever I am not currently eating sugar and fat," or "I promise to end the new year older than I am today."

## Rules for Unruly Families

If you ask me, the phrase "family rules" is an oxymoron not unlike "freezer burn," "unbiased opinion," or "jumbo shrimp": there's something self-contradictory about the phrase. This is because, quite frankly, families are downright unruly.

> *If you ask me, the phrase "family rules" is an oxymoron not unlike "freezer burn" or "jumbo shrimp": there's something self-contradictory about the phrase. This is because, quite frankly, families are downright unruly.*

Think about it: If family life were predictable, could I claim the experience of finding a half-eaten banana in my toothbrush drawer? Of course not.

If family life always ran according to plan, would I be watching *The Little Mermaid* at 3:00 A.M. with a toddler on a Dimetapp buzz? I don't think so.

If family life were organized, would my ten-year-old have slept in a sleeping bag last night because the bedsheets that went in the hamper last week have yet to see the inside of the washing machine? Never!

And yet, this is the environment into which we drop a slate of rules, and then wonder why they're about as effective as window screens in a submarine.

I don't know what it's like in your home, but at my house, rules related to chores, bedtime, spending money, and activities with friends seem to exist in a constant state of renegotiation.

Particularly at this stage in the game. My ten-year-old is maturing rapidly for her age. The other day she came home from school in tears. When I asked her what was wrong, she told

250

me through sobs that while carpooling home, she got smooshed between two balloons.

Come again?

That's right, balloons. It was Valentine's Day and the kids—Kaitlyn included—brought balloons home from school. And two of those seemingly innocuous rubber wonders apparently accosted my daughter and reduced her to the emotional equivalent of a wet sponge.

If you're a woman, you recognize the signs. I know I did.

HORMONES!

I hugged her and told her everything was okay. She wiped her eyes, brightened, and asked for a snack.

*If family life always ran according to plan, would I be watching* **The Little Mermaid** *at 3:00 A.M. with a toddler on a Dimetapp buzz? I don't think so.*

Yep. Hormones, alright. Imagine: Hormones *and* the terrible twos in the same house, at the same time. So much for family planning! And I hear it only gets wilder! Some of my friends have teenagers, and the stories they tell could be marketed as a form of birth control. I saw a bumper sticker once that said, "Parents of teenagers know why animals eat their young"—and some moms I know might agree!

Family life is unpredictable, unorganized, unplanned. It's not tidy. Foolproof directions are few and far between. More often than not, parents find themselves flying by the seat of their pants. And, to be honest, sometimes rules just get in the way. Maybe that's because family life isn't about regulations as much as it is about relationships. It's about asking questions like: "What are you feeling?" "How are you struggling?" "What are your needs right now?" and "How can I help you become all that God intended when he placed you in my life?"

If following the rules helps us do this, that's great. If they hinder, hurt, or hamper our efforts, then that's another story.

251

Sometimes, for example, bedtimes are less important than a heart-to-heart talk, even if it *is* 10:00 P.M. on a school night.

Maybe a weekend curfew needs to be renegotiated in light of a special date or event.

Perhaps Saturday chores should be nixed in order to take advantage of the gift of a February day that feels like spring.

*Family life isn't about regulations as much as it is about relationships.*

When I was growing up, we had family rules. We also knew when to break those rules. I remember my folks calling the Downey public school district to announce that my sisters and I wouldn't be in class that day—our family was going to brunch instead. I remember days when my parents canceled appointments and stayed home from work so they could spend the entire day sitting in the living room with a rebellious teen, hashing out issues until the conflict could resolve in a hug. I remember the day my dad scolded a chubby thirteen-year-old for eating a piece of candy before breakfast, and when he saw that his words hurt me, showed up hours later bearing a box of See's Candy Nuts and Chews with the inscription, "I may be a little 'nutty,' but I love you."

Sometimes, a rule is like a good tool: Use it when it builds and strengthens, but don't be afraid to set it aside if wielding it will cause destruction or scars.

## Rules to Live By

So far all I seem to have done is support the myth that rules are made to be broken. And yet . . .

It really is a myth, you know.

Despite all that I've said about bending the rules, there really are certain, inalienable principles that need to be honored—as consistently as humanly possible—for our families to thrive. Will we make mistakes? Sure. Will we fall short of perfection? Without a doubt. But the rules that follow . . . well . . . they're worth fighting to protect. Compromise on curfew if you have to. Renegotiate that earring ultimatum. Bend on bedtime. But approach the following principles with pit-bull resolve.

## Rule #1: *We will do whatever it takes to stay faithful to our marriage vows.*

If this principle is compromised, the destruction and fall-out can send family members reeling for years. Family life—as it existed before the betrayal—may die a painful death in divorce court. Or it may suffocate slowly under a mother lode of guilt and secret sin. Is there hope and healing after adultery? There can be—some marriages emerge stronger than before despite the scars. But the road to restoration can be a journey of many years and many tears. So stay faithful.

## Rule #2: *Family members must be respectful to each other at all times, even when angry or hurt.*

The world can be an abusive place. Ideally, your home should be a safe haven where family members can relax, re-group, and rejuvenate without fear of emotional, verbal, or physical violence. Will there be conflicts? Sure! Angry outbursts? No doubt! Rivalry and competition? Count on it!

Conflicts, anger, and rivalry need to be resolved. Don't be misled into thinking that you can achieve respect among family members by ignoring or denying conflicts. These dynamics exist in even the healthiest families. The key is to encourage the members of your family to talk about feelings, misunderstandings, and disagreements without devaluing anyone or inflicting wounds in the process. That means no profanity, no hitting or throwing, no name-calling, no screaming or tantrums, no insults or put-downs. Establish disciplinary procedures—time-outs, written and verbal apologies, or restricted privileges—to be followed when these guidelines are broken. Within these guidelines, any topic is permissible and every conflict worthy of discussion.

### Rule #3: It matters what we watch, listen to, and read.

We've all heard the phrase "garbage in, garbage out." If we put garbage into our hearts and minds, we will get garbage out via our words, actions, and attitudes. Every family's definition of "garbage" might be different: books, movies, and music allowed in one home might be off-limits in another. Wherever you draw the line, just draw one. Let your kids know that standards determining acceptable input are established by your family and not by their peers, the media, or the hottest new star or starlet. Teach your kids not to "go with the flow" of public opinion, but to use discernment when making choices regarding books, movies, and music.

### Rule #4: We learn from our mistakes and from the mistakes of others.

It's been said that the difference between smart people and dumb people is not that smart people never make mistakes, but that they don't keep making the same ones over and over again! An adult or child who is fearful of making a mistake will hesitate to try anything new, and growth will be hindered! If you try to teach your children to be perfect, you will have prepared them for failure, since perfection is unattainable. If you teach them to learn from their mistakes, you will have prepared them for success, having given them the power to transform the many inevitable mistakes of life into stepping-stones.

Encourage the mastering of new skills and challenges. Applaud success. Applaud failures too; don't overreact in the face of a mistake, but use the experience to teach wisdom or to praise any positive character traits that were highlighted during the experience. Never use words, body language, or laughter to demean. And above all, glean anything positive that you can from your own mistakes; kids learn best by our example.

### Rule #5: We observe a mandatory daily quota of hugs and "I love yous."

Physical and verbal affirmation are hard to overdo. The human touch is a powerful healing agent. Just today Kaitlyn came home from school crying over imagined slights and snubs from peers and friends (which can be, by the way, even more painful than actual snubs!). We talked for half an hour in my office, to no avail. She remained as convinced as ever that she was unlovable. I finally did what I should have done from the beginning: walked her into the den, snuggled onto the couch, and rocked her in my arms.

This, of course, is easier said than done. At ten, Kaitlyn is a small adult. She wears the same size shoe as me, and six inches from now we'll be standing eye to eye. Still, we rocked. We didn't say much. For a few moments I sang a lullaby I used to sing when she was a baby, but mostly we were silent. I stroked her hair and patted her back as we rocked. Twenty minutes later she chirped off to the phone to call a girlfriend, then watched the Flintstones on TV. Right now she is singing and playing the piano as I write.

My friend Linda has two sons at home, ages nineteen and twenty-three. Despite tumultuous teen years, conflict, and growing pains, the boys readily exchange affectionate gestures and words with their mother. Linda says, "As your children struggle to find themselves and leave the nest, it's easy to look back and see things you wish you had done differently as a parent. But one of the things I can see that I did right was reminding my kids daily, verbally and physically, how much I value them and what a pleasure it is to have them in my life. The affirmation and affection we've shared through the years has bolstered us through tremendous conflict. It has provided a connection that has weathered significant storms. Both of my boys are over six feet tall. But they'll still sit on my lap and tell me about their day, or give me a hug and say 'I love you, Mom,' in front of their macho friends. And I know I did okay. I did something right, and it shows."

### Rule #6: Bend a child's will to conform to a rule; but bend the rule before breaking a child's spirit.

So how do we know? When it comes to family rules, when do we hold fast and when do we let up? We want the rules to make our kids feel guided and secure . . . but rules can also stifle and provoke. Is it possible to maintain the right balance?

Not without help.

The fact is, you and I are flawed and fallible. We're not rocket scientists. We're not mind readers. We're just average Janes and Joes stumbling blindly through this parenting thing, reading books, watching Oprah, gleaning parenting tips here and there, and doing the best we can day by day.

The good news is that there's someone we can go to for help. A father himself who knows this parenting thing inside out. He's raised good kids and some holy terrors as well. He knows precisely when to lay down the law and when to dole out the grace. Best yet, he's ready and waiting to help us become better parents, imparting wisdom, insights, and guidance the moment we ask.

You know who it is, don't you? The Ultimate Father, the Creator of us all.

I'd like to tell you a story. It's a story about a dad, his son, and the heavenly Father who loves them both.

Mark Bellinger begins each morning in prayer, kneeling by the living room couch, talking to God about the day's events and about each member of his family.

One Saturday morning, however, Mark found it hard to concentrate. It was the morning after he had put his seventeen-year-old son Craig on restriction for breaking curfew. The house was quiet, and Mark's prayer time should have gone smoothly. But as he prayed he couldn't shake the sense that God was sending him a disturbing message. He became convinced that God was asking him to reverse Craig's restriction!

Mark dismissed the feeling and tried to continue with his prayers. But as he prayed for wisdom as a parent, he again felt the Holy Spirit stirring in his soul. God was saying: "You just finished praying for wisdom, but you're not listening to me!"

Mark remembers: "I argued with God. I told him I never go back on my word, especially when it comes to discipline, and my kids know it. I'm not harsh, but I'm fair, and a rule is a rule. But that day, the feeling wouldn't go away. God wanted Craig off restriction."

Mark called Craig into the living room. Perplexed, he shook his head. "Son, this'll be a first," he said slowly. "As I was praying, I felt God telling me to let you off restriction. He told me

*If you try to teach your children to be perfect, you will have prepared them for failure, since perfection is unattainable. If you teach them to learn from their mistakes, you will have prepared them for success, having given them the power to transform the many inevitable mistakes of life into stepping-stones.*

257

to tell you that he overruled my decision. He told me that I'm the head of this house, but that he's the head of me."

Craig didn't whoop or cheer. Instead, his eyes welled with tears. "Dad, I know how you are about rules. I knew you wouldn't change your mind, so I didn't say anything, but this weekend is the church youth retreat and I really wanted to go. So I stayed up half the night praying that God would speak to you. I knew that if it was his will for me to go to the retreat, he would somehow let you change your mind and let me go."

When do we lay down the law? When do we hand out the grace? God knows our kids better than we do. He loves them with a love we can't even fathom. Read the advice and common sense he's prepared for you in his written Word. Ask him to make your heart sensitive to his gentle nudgings, your spirit sensitive to his whispered wisdom. If you don't know him as a heavenly Father, but merely as a higher power, spiritual force, or cosmic being, then begin by telling him you want to be able to approach him as *his* child, so you can then approach him for *your* child. How do you become a child of God? I outlined the steps back in chapter seven, on page 94. Your adoption into the family of the living God is a simple prayer away!

Rules: Executed in love, tempered with grace, honed by prayer, they can protect and safeguard your family like little else!

# The Best Things in Life Are Free

 verybody likes to get something for nothing. I joined a book club once because I could get five books for a dollar. Turns out I wasn't allowed to quit the club until I had purchased a number of books equivalent to the inventory of the Library of Congress.

Then there was the summer Larry and I came across a really good deal. We were vacationing in Florida and someone told us we could receive two tickets to Disneyworld absolutely FREE OF CHARGE. All we had to do to claim our tickets was listen politely to a thirty-minute presentation on time-share condos.

Of course, our first clue that something was wrong with this picture should have been the fact that, as we pulled our car into the parking lot, the only people we saw leaving the building had two-day stubble. The experience began pleasantly enough, but our presenter was obviously truth impaired when

*Does raising a family mean certain costs and sacrifices? If you want to talk costs, talk to the new mother who craves sleep the way talk show hosts crave ratings.*

he told us we would be done before lunchtime. Unless, of course, he meant lunchtime the following Thursday.

As it turned out, what we really had to do to get our free tickets was sit through two and a half hours of pressure that rapidly escalated to browbeating and intensified from there. Organized crime should take a lesson from these guys. I think the salesperson's parting shot to my husband was, "I can't believe you call yourself a business professor and you can't even make a simple decision like this one." Of course, he was ignoring the fact that we weren't having trouble making a decision—we were just having trouble making the decision he wanted to hear.

In any case, we got our passes to Disneyworld. But they were hardly free. What we paid for blood pressure medication and psychotherapy rapidly exceeded the retail value of the two tickets.

## There's No Such Thing as a Free Lunch

I guess there's no such thing as a free lunch. But we can still dream, can't we?

We'd all love to get that lucky break. Win the lottery. Experience a windfall. Don't tell me your heart didn't skip a beat the very first time you got a letter from Ed McMahon announcing that you had just won a million dollars. Unfortunately, life doesn't usually work that way.

There's this school of thought, however, that says life offers plenty of freebies. Indeed, this philosophy states that the best things in life are free. But I'm not so sure about that. In fact, the *very* best things—a strong and passionate marriage . . . transparent and intimate friendships . . . the respect of our children . . . a vibrant relationship with our Creator—exact a heavy toll. They may be priceless, but they are not without cost.

Does raising a family mean certain costs and sacrifices?

Has Don King ever had a bad hair day?

If you want to talk costs, talk to the new mother who craves sleep the way talk show hosts crave ratings. Talk to the dad who gives up playoff tickets to attend a piano recital. Last week I flew to California to visit my folks. Counting both flights, I spent a total of seven hours wedged into a seat the size of a milk carton, wrestling with a twenty-four-pound "lap" child who contains about as easily as an octopus. Now if that's not paying a price, I don't know what is.

And yet . . .

Let's talk about rewards. If you want to know about rewards, go ahead: Talk to the mother who would rather get a full-night's sleep than win the lottery. Talk to the dad who has no problem catching z's for eight consecutive hours each night; he just wishes he could do so without hearing "Heart and Soul" in his sleep. Talk to the toddler-toting woman deboarding Flight 307 with peanuts in her hair, Coke stains down the front of her blouse, and her sanity in a body bag.

*My mom and I drove past the houses we lived in while I was growing up: the house on Birchdale where I got my first puppy, the house on Samoline where I got my first kiss, and the house on Farm Street where I got my wings and flew away.*

I dare you. Ask them about the rewards. Ask them if it's worth the price. You know what they'll say, don't you? The same thing you and I would say.

It's worth it all.

This past week, in California, I revisited my childhood. This came about because, several weeks ago, my parents moved back to the town where I grew up. Talk about a trip down memory lane! The day I got into town, my parents, my daughters, and I ate breakfast at Foxy's Restaurant, the same restaurant where my family often went for hot chocolate after church on Sunday nights . . . the same restaurant where, at eighteen, I told my folks I had just been in a car accident and my car was now a modern art sculpture . . . the same restaurant where Larry and I sat and watched my parents' faces register bewilderment, shock, and then glee as a waitress served coffee in cups adorned with baby rattles as our way of announcing the conception of their first grandchild.

**Characterized by heartache and hilarity and all that comes between, family life provides us with passion and purpose like nothing else.**

Later in the week, my mom and I drove past the houses we lived in while I was growing up: the house on Birchdale where I got my first puppy, the house on Samoline where I got my first kiss, and the house on Farm Street where I got my wings and flew away.

Then there was the afternoon my sister Michelle, her husband, Russ, and I took my girls to the park we frequented most as children. Most of the old toys had been replaced, but the memories were still there. I sat on the patch of grass where my mother had once spread a blanket and read to us from *Huckleberry Finn*. I revisited the community art gallery that had once displayed a papier-mâché sculpture I'd made in summer school. I saw the basketball courts where my sister Renee and I often loitered in the hopes of meeting boys.

The week seemed ripe with memories, the air heavy with their scent as old shadows and stories, bygone triumphs and tragedies, and remembered angst and adventure beckoned sweetly at every turn.

Family life. What a wonderful phrase! Indeed, where there is family, there is life. Raising our kids, loving our spouses, enjoying the parents and siblings and grandparents with whom we've shared so much, this is life at its very best. Do the best things in life come our way without a price? Nope. But maybe that's okay. The price we pay is just a token, really, in light of the priceless value we receive in return. Indeed, the payment is exceeded by the prize, the pain eclipsed by the poignant beauty inherent in the privilege of belonging to a family.

In the previous pages we've covered a lot of ground, you and I, talking about everything from lethal lunch box leftovers to apology faux pas to etiquette for tardy spouses. We've talked about postnatal bodies and Brillo pads and how to restrain a toddler with a dog leash. We've laughed and learned and laid bare more than a few myths about what it means to raise a family in the '90s and beyond.

And in the process, maybe we've been reminded of something that's not a myth, something that deserves a prominent place in our minds as we seek to balance all the demands that love and duty conspire to throw our way. The fact is this: Family life is a gift. Characterized by heartache and hilarity and all that comes between, it provides us with passion and purpose like nothing else. Regardless of the stage your family is in, cherish these days. It doesn't get any better than this.

# What women are saying about *Pillow Talk*...

"Recently I heard you speaking about *Pillow Talk* on our local Christian radio station. By the end of the broadcast, I was in my car in search of the book, which I am reading for a second time."

—Kathy in Ohio

"I've been married 31 years and have two daughters. I read your book while driving on a road trip with my husband. I laughed all the way from Texas to Mississippi, and gained a whole new perspective on sex. I can't wait to pass the book on to my married daughter!"

—Ann in Texas

"I just finished reading *Pillow Talk*. I laughed and cried. At certain places in the book, I felt as if I knew you! I want to wait about a month and read it again. I don't want to make the same mistakes the second time around."

—Janet in South Carolina

"If you're looking for a great book on marriage to give to a friend (or read for yourself) you won't want to miss *Pillow Talk* by Karen Linamen. Her refreshing honesty, practical and gutsy topics, and real-life stories will give you a wider perspective on your own marriage—and make you chuckle, too!"

—Ramona Cramer Tucker
Editor of *Today's Christian Woman* magazine

# *Pillow Talk*
# Table of Contents

# More praise for
# *Pillow Talk...*

"My husband and I are just shy of our second anniversary. Your book answered many questions that I had about sexual relations with my husband! I also enjoyed how you created a friendship bond with your readers! Thank you for writing such a wonderful book."

—Julie in Georgia

"I laughed out loud while reading the book so many times that my husband actually stopped watching TV and told me he wanted to read the book as soon as I was finished with it!"

—Monica in Texas

> "My husband told me he can't wait until you write your next book. I said, 'Why? You haven't even read this one yet.' He said, 'I don't need to read it—I'm already reaping the benefits!'"
>
> —Darla in Texas

"My husband and I have been married for 17 years and I knew I needed to tune up my part in the romance department! Your book was easy to read, applicable, and tremendously humorous. As you know, women are quite verbal about their relationships, and I find that many of my peers are in a similar dilemma with a fading desire for physical intimacy. Thank you for writing this book. I plan on passing it around."

—Evelyn in Missouri

# What Readers Are Saying about
## *Happily Ever After...*

"Karen Linamen's new book is magic! I really enjoyed the chapter entitled 'You Can't Get Pregnant While Breast-Feeding.' I loved how she got readers past the mundane, everyday facets of mothering and helped us recognize and recapture the magic inherent in what we do."

—Nancy in Indiana

"I often found myself laughing out loud. Best yet, the humor is laced with truths that encourage and uplift. After I read about 'New Motivations for Tired Homemakers' I actually got up and cleaned my house! Now, *that's* effective!"

—Traci in Minnesota

"Karen's observations on the post-natal body were hilarious. I thought to myself, 'Finally, a woman who tells it like it is!' There were so many places I laughed aloud, my ten-year-old asked me what was so funny."

—Jackie in Washington

"You manage to take mundane events like changing diapers and making bag lunches and somehow make it all seem glamorous and even hysterical. I hate to admit this, but I laughed so hard in places that I wet my pants! You did a beautiful job creating a book that is very funny and very honest as well."

—Marci in Michigan

"I loved the way little nuggets of truth are squeezed in there with all the fun. The humor is so real because it's about stuff we all go through. It makes me feel better to know I'm not the only mom who is shortsighted at times . . . who cries at tender moments . . . or who has survived a rambunctious child in a restaurant!"

—Darla in New Jersey

"The pages I read not only brimmed with humorous anecdotes, but also provided a sense of understanding and acceptance of the traits that make us all so different."

—Jeffie in Texas

"What a great book! I was howling. The book is funny and real, regardless of where your experiences of family life come from. I don't have any children, but I certainly have memories from my childhood. And reading the book, I gained a much better picture of what to expect when I have my own family! Karen lets you know that even though life is far from picture-perfect, it's still worthy of celebration."

—Michelle in California

"Oh, yeah. Been there, done that, got the tee shirt. I'm 57 years old, five children, ten grandchildren. I laughed, I cried, I had memories stirred that were lost in time. Young mothers will know they're not alone; grandmothers will recall precious memories."

—Donna in Texas

"I loved it! Time after time, I found my own experiences mirrored in the pages I was reading, and ended up laughing as a result. It's so encouraging to know that other people have been through the same things. What a wonderful book!"

—Sharon in Texas

"I just couldn't put it down. I laughed through some parts, and cried through others. Karen is so honest and down-to-earth—every age-group will relate to what she has written. It doesn't matter if you had a baby six months ago, six years ago, or sixty years ago—*Happily Ever After* is about things you just don't forget."

—Peggy in Mississippi

Karen Linamen is a freelance writer and popular speaker for women's groups. A former editor with Focus on the Family, she has written or cowritten seven books and several hundred articles. She loves hearing from readers! To reach her, write:

Karen Linamen
P.O. Box 2673
Duncanville, Texas 75138

E-mail:
klinamen@flash.net